BROADCASTING
THE CANADIAN WAY

By ALBERT A. SHEA

Canada 1980

World Communications **(UNESCO)**

Culture In Canada

Etc.

albert a. shea

broadcasting the canadian way

 harvest house montreal

First Edition August 1963

Library of Congress Catalog Card Number: 63-19560

The cover design is by Heiner Hegemann

Printed by The Runge Press Ltd., Ottawa

CONTENTS

Acknowledgments

Foreword

ACKNOWLEDGMENTS

A debt is acknowledged to the Canadian Broadcasting League which commissioned the author to do an objective study of "Basic Issues in Broadcasting". That study was the point of departure for the present work. Although the author alone is responsible for the facts and the point of view expressed in this book, scores of people whose experience in broadcasting makes their views especially helpful have been consulted in the course of its preparation. The principal individuals who contributed in this way are:

R. E. Misener, CFCF Radio and TV, Canadian Marconi, Montreal

Robert M. Fowler, Pulp & Paper Institute, Montreal

Pat Pearce, *Montreal Star*

CBC, Ottawa—Alphonse Ouimet

> Frank Peers
>
> Orville Shugg
>
> Eugene Hallman
>
> Andrew Cowan
>
> W. A. Macdonald
>
> Arthur Laird, Research

Herbert Steinhouse, CBC, Montreal

Stuart Griffiths, CJOH-TV, Ottawa

Arthur Dupont, founder of CJAD, Montreal

Dr. Eugene Forsey, Canadian Labour Congress, former governor, BBG

Mrs. Gladys Coke Musson, Kingston

Dr. Roby Kidd, Social Science Research Council of Canada, Ottawa

David Kirk, Canadian Federation of Agriculture

Guy Fournier, President, *Fédération des Auteurs et des Artistes du Canada*

Pierre Boucher, President, *Union des Artistes de Montreal*
 BBG, Ottawa—Dr. Andrew Stewart
                    Ross McLean, programs
                    Dr. John Dawson, economist
                    Dr. W. Hull (University of Manitoba)
 James Allard, Canadian Association of Broadcasters
 CTV, Toronto—Spence W. Caldwell
                    Gordon Keeble
 Allan Thomas, Canadian Association for Adult Education
 Adèle Lauzon, *Le Magazine Maclean*
 Robert Fulford, *Maclean's Magazine*
 Neil Morrison, York University (former Director of Research, CBC)
 Samuel Elber, Editor, *Canadian Sponsor*

In the few instances where persons interviewed have expressed a desire to remain anonymous, I have respected their wishes.

FOREWORD

FOREWORD

SOMETHING OF VALUE

Canada has a highly diversified population, thinly scattered across a broad continent. To provide contact and encourage mutual understanding a coherent system of communications is essential. The Canadian nation relies heavily on the public communication organization, the Canadian Broadcasting Corporation (CBC), known as *Radio Canada* to the audiences of the French networks. Many Canadians have learned to place a high value on CBC–*Radio Canada*. We have good reasons for wanting to keep our characteristic broadcasting institution strong and independent.

In addition to the CBC, private broadcasting in both radio and television, is now a permanent part of the Canadian scene. For many years the private broadcasters lived in fear that all broadcasting stations in Canada would be nationalized. Then, as it became more apparent that private broadcasting was here to stay, the private broadcasters spent a number of years in fear, more vocal than real, of being pushed around by the CBC. For the CBC, in addition to operating the national network service, was also responsible for regulating the private sector of broadcasting. In 1958, all that changed. The private broadcasters succeeded in the prolonged campaign to obtain what they called "a neutral referee". They argued, with some reason, that they could not compete with the CBC, and also be regulated by their principal competitor.

In 1958, a new Broadcasting Act brought into being an entirely new and separate regulatory body, the Board of Broadcast Governors (BBG). If the private broadcasters and their friends are happy with the results, the CBC and their friends are not. There is a battle going on now about networks. Should stations linked with the CBC network be allowed to depart and join the private CTV network?

xi

Should the CBC build more stations so that it does not have to depend on privately-owned stations for distribution of the national programs? Should the CBC drop all commercial broadcasts, and give up the revenue which they earn?

Then, there is the sad story of the Grey Cup controversy. Behind the smoke and heat of that controversy, and beneath the fog in which it expired on December 1, 1962, there lay an unresolved conflict. This time it was not just the traditional conflict between the private and the public sectors of broadcasting. There was disagreement between two official organizations, both created by, and responsible to, the Parliament of Canada.

The abiding tension between the BBG—the Board of Broadcast Governors, and the CBC—the Canadian Broadcasting Corporation, is *not* over who is boss. By law, the BBG is the final authority on broadcasting matters. But, the CBC has its own job to do, its own responsibilities to the people of Canada and to Parliament. A battle is being waged over *how far* the BBG should be allowed to go in telling the CBC how to do its job.

That the CBC has survived many crises during the past quarter-century is no ground for complacency. The CBC has survived only because there have been people, even prior to the establishment of its predecessor, the Canadian Radio Broadcasting Commission, in 1933, who believed in the importance to Canada of a national broadcasting service. These people have fought, lobbied, given their time, energy and resources for three decades to bring into being and maintain a system dedicated to serving the information, entertainment and cultural needs of all Canadians, regardless of language, region, or political persuasion. To survive and improve, the CBC has always had to place its responsibility to the Canadian people ahead of the concerns and pressures of the advertiser and the party politician.

Private broadcasting has its friends, too. It provides much useful service and has good potential to serve Canadians. If we look to the experience of the United States, Great Britain, and other countries, there seems little doubt, however, that it is primarily to the publicly-owned CBC that we must continue to turn for a broadcasting service which will nourish a growing Canadian cultural identity. To form a nation at all, with our vast extent of geography and our diversity of peoples, has required Canadians to make imaginative and heroic efforts in communication, as well as in transportation.

It is no exaggeration to say that the survival of Canada depends on making use of modern communication to maintain the integrity and unity of the nation. Our considerable dependence, both economic and cultural, on our powerful neighbour, the United States has its virtues, but also makes us vulnerable to the core of our national personality. For Canadians who speak English, as well as for those who are French speaking, CBC-*Radio Canada* is the principal instrument of communication available to provide the means of cultural survival. It can also serve as the link that will enable English- and French-speaking Canadians to remain united.

I

THE BASIC ISSUE

THE BASIC ISSUE

There has been a public broadcasting organization in Canada for some thirty years, since the establishment of the Canadian Radio Broadcasting Commission in 1933.

The present Canadian Broadcasting Corporation was established in 1936, and celebrated its 25th anniversary in 1961. The television activities of the CBC began in September, 1952; the 10th anniversary of TV in Canada was celebrated in 1962.

Four volumes serve as landmarks in the history of broadcasting. All are reports by Royal Commissions. They are the *Aird Commission Report* of 1929; *The Massey Commission Report* of 1951, in which broadcasting was studied as part of a broad investigation into the state of the arts, letters and sciences in Canada; *The Fowler Commission Report* of 1957; and *The Glassco Commission Report* of 1962-63, which was concerned with the question of efficiency of operation in all government organizations, including the CBC.

The problems of broadcasting have also been studied by some 16 Parliamentary Committees, on an average of about once every two years, and most recently in 1961.

Yet, today there is real concern about the state of broadcasting in Canada. This concern has been expressed on all sides: by private broadcasters, the CTV Network, representatives of the Canadian Association of Broadcasters, by officials of the Board of Broadcast Governors, by the Canadian Broadcasting Corporation, by national citizens' organizations represented in the Canadian Broadcasting League, as well as by individual journalists, scholars and citizens who are sensitive to the important role of broadcasting in our national life.

What has gone wrong?

Basically there is confusion, disagreement and open conflict between the various elements involved in broadcasting because of the lack of common understanding and agreement as to the aims and purposes of broadcasting. There is really only one *basic* issue, to which all others are related: *What are the aims and purposes of broadcasting in Canada, and how can broadcasting best be organized to achieve these objectives?*

There have been times in the past when this central issue was apparently settled. Now, once again the air must be cleared, and we must reach an intelligent answer to this question.

Broadcasting has been a constant battleground. As long as radio and television remain important influences in our lives, and as long as vital financial and ideological stakes are involved, broadcasting will continue to be the cause of much controversy. There was however, fairly general agreement from 1929 until recent times as to what Canadians expected from broadcasting.

In 1929, Sir John Aird, Chairman of the first Royal Commission on broadcasting, said that broadcasting "can be adequately served only by some form of public ownership, operation and control behind which is the national power and prestige of the whole public of the Dominion of Canada."

In 1932, the Rt. Hon. R. B. Bennett, prime minister of Canada, stated: "Canadians have the right to a system of broadcasting from Canadian sources equal in all respects to that of any other country . . . this country must be assured of complete Canadian control of broadcasting from Canadian sources, free from foreign interference or influence."

The principle of a national broadcasting service, of Canadian broadcasting for Canadians, and the recognition of the need to meet the expense which this involved from public funds, was reaffirmed in many statements by government leaders and Parliamentary Committees. The principle was reaffirmed for television by the 1950 Parliamentary Committee:

Such a system linking together Canadians in all parts of the country and broadcasting a large volume of material produced by Canadians is of great importance to the people of Canada as a whole . . . It is obviously in the national interest that television in Canada should be essentially Canadian . . . and that it carry in large proportion Canadian material, produced by Canadians. . . . Such a development will undoubtedly be more expensive. . . .
(Your Committee) does see the need for the establishment of some proper and adequate system of financing Canadian television development in the general national interest.

Other Parliamentary Committees reaffirmed the view that while television is undoubtedly complex and costly, it is highly important in developing and maintaining Canadian identity and unity.

Current difficulties can best be discussed by starting with the findings of *The Fowler Commission Report,* in 1957. The difficulties, however, are not in the findings of that Royal Commission, but in the circumstance that the Broadcasting Act of 1958, and subsequent actions, have largely ignored and reversed the findings of *The Fowler Commission Report.*

The principle that at one time appeared to be established, and which had been frequently reaffirmed—that the primary and essential element in Canadian broadcasting must be a national broadcasting service—is once again being questioned and attacked.

Our national broadcasting service has the task of making full use of the fabulous powers of radio and television to enrich the lives of Canadians with entertainment and information. To perform this task adequately, it must be safeguarded against two influences which could diminish or destroy the value of its efforts: politics and commercialism. This is not to imply that the national service can have nothing to do with political or commercial matters. But it does imply that no politician and no corporation or advertiser should be allowed to interfere with the national service in the carrying out of its extremely important responsibilities to the Canadian people.

The Fowler Royal Commission recommended the appointment of a body to be known as the Board of Broadcast Governors. It said: "The Board is charged with the supervision, regulation and control of all broadcasting in Canada in the public interest."

We now have a body in Canada, called the Board of Broadcast Governors, established by the Broadcasting Act of 1958. This is how the Act describes the objects and purposes of the Board:

The Board shall, for the purpose of ensuring the continued existence and efficient operation of a national broadcasting system and the provision of a varied and comprehensive broadcasting service of a high standard that is basically Canadian in content and character, regulate the establishment and operation of networks of broadcasting stations, the activities of public and private broadcasting stations in Canada and the relationship between them and provide for the final determination of all matters and questions in relation thereto.

But, the essential point is that the present Board of Broadcast Governors is *not* the Board recommended by the Fowler Royal Commission.

The Fowler Report recommended that in Canada there should be only *one* Board for the regulation of broadcasting. It recommended that the Canadian Broadcasting Corporation should submit its annual report to this Board, which in turn would submit it to Parliament. It recommended that the CBC should have a President and a General Manager, but *no* Board either of Governors or Directors.

The Fowler Report recommended that in the first instance the President and General Manager should be appointed, and their salaries fixed, by the Governor in Council, which, is an old-fashioned way of saying, by the government of the day. But, on subsequent occasions, the

President and General Manager of the CBC would be appointed, and their salaries fixed, by the Board of Broadcast Governors with the approval of the Governor in Council.

According to *The Fowler Report,* there would be only one body of citizens responsible to Parliament for the operations of the CBC, and of private broadcasting. Instead, the Broadcasting Act of 1958, in addition to providing what it also called a Board of Broadcast Governors, provided that the CBC should have a President, a Vice-President and nine other directors, appointed by the Governor in Council. The CBC, as well as the BBG, is required to report to Parliament, through the responsible Minister of the Crown.

The BBG we now have is not the BBG recommended in The Fowler Report.

The Fowler Report concluded that all broadcasting in Canada must be treated as one system, and that only one body should be in over-all control, and should report to Parliament on the operation of this system.

The Fowler Report states:

We have accepted the concept that there is only one broadcasting system in Canada, with services to the Canadian people provided by a combination of public and private stations, all of which are integral parts of that single system. For such a system there is nothing unsound or improper in having Parliament delegate powers of supervision and control over the operations of all Canadian broadcasters to a single body of representative Canadian men and women.

The Fowler Report then proceeds to provide a warning, which now reads like an amazingly accurate prediction, of the difficulties which will arise if *two* boards are established:

But suppose . . . we had the two boards set up today: one a board to supervise the operations of the CBC, the other a board to regulate and control the operations of both CBC and private stations and to deal with licensing matters. By definition, the regulatory board would be required to know a great deal about the CBC, to follow its growth and development and to take the public interest in the CBC into

account in its decisions. The two boards, composed of people of similar background and qualifications, operating in many of the same fields and necessarily in close contact with each other would either draw together or pull apart. If all were harmonious between them, if they generally thought alike and agreed with each other, the situation would quickly become indistinguishable from that existing today; except that it would be more cumbersome to have a double review of many issues and more expensive to the taxpayer.
Alternatively, if the two bodies (as is probably more likely) pulled apart, one or other would be bound to assert dominance, through the skill and strength of personality of its members, especially of its chairman. If the CBC Board became dominant, the regulatory body would tend to become a cipher; it would be an extra expense and formality to approve, generally, what the CBC wanted. On the other hand, if the regulatory body became dominant, and the real centre of power, the CBC Board would become unimportant, and real control would be exercised over both the CBC and the private stations as well. As far as the management of the CBC was concerned it would be frustrated; as far as control was concerned it would probably become a more active and onerous regulation of private stations by the body interested in and dominating the CBC—the very basis of the present complaint. As a practical matter, we do not believe you can have two administrative bodies, appointed by the same government and with similar personnel involved in the regulation of broadcasting, without having duplication of expense and effort, undesirable friction between the two, and a loss of efficiency.

This describes, with astonishing accuracy, what we are experiencing as a result of having two administrative bodies: a Board of Broadcast Governors, and a CBC complete with its own Board of Directors, each responsible, and reporting separately, to Parliament. We have needless expense, we have undesirable friction, we have a serious loss of efficiency.

Another key recommendation of *The Fowler Report,* also ignored, was that the Parliament should assure the CBC a regular annual income over a period of five years at least, by means of a statutory grant. This would enable the CBC to plan its long-range activities on some reasonable basis, it would remove the year-to-year uncertainty, as well as the danger of political influence on the activities of the Corporation, which are present when it must make an annual application to Parliament for funds, both for capital and operating purposes. The British Broadcasting Corporation enjoys this type of financing, and has for many years. Many groups and individuals in Canada have urged the importance of removing the CBC from the difficulties and dangers of dependence on a yearly application to Parliament for funds. As matters stand, the CBC must still go to Parliament each year to obtain the funds it requires, over and above the commercial revenue which it earns. While Parliament has the power of approval, it is the party in power that controls money bills and determines the size of the annual grant to the CBC.

The Fowler Report described broadcasting in Canada as a single system, with public and private stations as integral parts. All its recommendations were designed to maintain the concept of a single system.

In a talk delivered in Ottawa in December, 1962, the president of the CBC, Mr. Alphonse Ouimet, compared the other broadcasting systems of the world with that of Canada:

The best way to understand the present complexity of the Canadian system is to compare it with the relative simplicity of other systems in existence today.

Broadcasting in the world today has two basic forms and various combinations of the two. On the one hand you have the purely or primarily public service approach, as found in most countries of Europe. On the other, you have the purely or primarily commercial approach, as typified by the United States system.

The American system is a model of simplicity—if not of public service. You have one authority—the FCC, which corresponds roughly to the Department of Transport in the Canadian system, and then you have the stations regulated by it. No conflict exists between public agencies, because there is no publicly-owned organization. There is no conflict of motive because each commercial station or each commercial network is operated as a business for the primary purpose of earning dividends for its shareholders. The public service motive is also present in varying degrees, but always within the limits imposed by commercial and business exigencies—it is the secondary motive.

Then you have the European systems. Here, although the concept is different, the systems are simple in the sense that they have very few elements and no difficult inter-relations. In most cases, you have a licensing authority, such as the Post Office, and a publicly-owned agency responsible for the provision of the national service. There are no private stations. Some of these organizations are completely independent of politics; others, unfortunately, are not; but the systems themselves are simple.

Then you have various mixtures of the commercial and public service approach. First, there are the publicly-owned monopolies who supplement their licence revenue through commercial operations, such as the RAI in Italy, PRIT in Poland and the SABC which operates both networks in South Africa—one commercial, the other non-commercial. Again, the organizational pattern is very simple.

Then you have the dual systems, such as the television system in Great Britain. There, they have the BBC, the publicly-owned public service which is a non-commercial organization and the ITA, the Independent Television Authority, responsible for commercial operations. I won't take time to explain just how ITA operates; anyone who has read the Pilkington Report will already know that it should not be taken as a model. The BBC is a publicly-owned organization established by Royal Charter, it is financed through licence fees, carries no advertising and is completely autonomous with respect to its programming and internal administration. It is responsible to Parliament and its operations are examined every ten years by a special Committee, set up by Parliament prior to the renewal of its Charter. It is self-sufficient in every way, the scale of its revenues is set by Parliament for a long period, it has all the facilities it requires for the production of programs and it owns and operates all the stations it requires for the distribution of its programs to the nation. The BBC, like the CBC, has only one "raison d'être"—to serve the public.

The British system is a simple dual system, with only two elements, BBC and ITA, both self-sufficient, both self-regulating with undivided, direct responsibility to Parliament. There is no separate regulatory Board in the British system.

Another good example of a simple, dual system is the Australian system. First, there is the publicly-owned ABC, the Australian Broadcasting Commission, which has the responsibility to provide the national service in radio and television, and which is financed through licences and carries no advertising. It has its own outlets, and therefore operates entirely independently of any privately-owned stations. In parallel with the ABC service, you have the commercial service which also has its own outlets and its own networks. The two services operate side by side and they have no inter-relations, except again that they compete for the same audience.

There is a regulatory board in Australia, but in practice it has little, if anything, to do with the ABC, the publicly-owned service except on technical matters.

On several grounds, Mr. Ouimet finds the Canadian system more complex and less satisfactory than other broadcasting systems. The CBC is not self-sufficient; to cover many parts of the country it is dependent on privately-owned commercial affiliates. Unlike the BBC, the CBC is no longer self-regulating. The CBC is responsible to Parliament, but it is also subject to BBG regulation. Unlike the BBC, the CBC is considerably dependent on commercial revenues. And, where the planning and finance of the BBC is on a long-term basis, under its 10-year charter, the CBC must operate on a year-to-year basis.

Evidence is growing that we are moving in the direction of a double system. Britain has a double system; so does Australia. But is a double system what we want and need in Canada?

There is now a private television network, CTV, which in January, 1963, included 9 member stations. CTV has plans to expand its network, and to increase its coverage of the Canadian television audience. The CBC, concerned about the possible loss of private affiliate stations which now serve as part of its national television network, is taking steps to secure CBC-owned television stations at key locations in each province.

In a speech delivered in December, 1962, the President of the CBC, Mr. Alphonse Ouimet, said: "I think that both the CBC and the private stations would be far more flexible in their operation, and the public would thus be better served, if CBC were able to provide the full national service through CBC-owned stations to all Canadians."

Mr. Ouimet emphasized that this was a very long-term suggestion. The CBC recognizes its indebtedness to many private stations for the role they have played as part of the national service. Their facilities will continue to be needed for a long time, according to Mr. Ouimet, but by a slow and gradual process he would like to see the public and private skeins of broadcasting unravelled and separated completely.

What is good for Britain may not be good for Canada. Even in Britain the 1962 Pilkington Commission found many faults with the British double system that stand in need of correction. Some observers feel that the double system in Australia has resulted in the triumph of the private, commercial broadcasters and the defeat of the national public broadcasting service.

Canada's tomorrows will unquestionably call for different solutions to our broadcasting problems than those applied during our yesterdays. The argument used by Mr. Ouimet that the present mixed system is too complex, that things would be a lot simpler with two completely separate systems, may not be a sufficient reason to abandon the single system. Broadcasting itself is a most complex form of communication. Our times may require that we cope with complex institutions, tough though they are to manage, rather than escape into alternatives which appear to be simple, but may, nevertheless, be unsatisfactory.

Present difficulties stem in part from the Broadcasting Act of 1958, and from the failure to clearly define the nature and limits of the authority and responsibility of the BBG and of the CBC. But, there would be problems, even if this central problem was resolved. Radio grew rapidly into an important medium of communication. During the past decade radio has been overshadowed by television, which is growing much more rapidly, and is an even more potent form of communication.

According to the Canadian advertising trade paper, *Marketing,* gross advertising revenues for 1962 are estimated at $633,700,000, accounting for 1.6 per cent of Canada's Gross National Product. More than half this sum went to periodicals, with daily newspapers accounting for close to 60 per cent of the dollars earned by periodicals. Television was on the rise, receiving 11 per cent of the total. The share of radio for 1962 was 9.3 per cent of the total. Outdoor advertising accounted for seven per cent. While newspapers continue to attract the largest share of advertising dollars, television is now in second place among the media and takes a larger slice of advertising revenue each year.

Not all private broadcasting stations show large profits. In fact, a number of the private television stations incurred substantial losses in their first year or two of operation. But, both radio and television stations, particularly in the main cities of Canada, are, at present, or potentially, capable of earning substantial profits on the money invested by the license holders.

Private profit and public service are not necessarily incompatible. But the evidence suggests that the use of radio and television to sell goods rarely is combined with a high standard of quality, variety and Canadian content in programming.

Both public and private broadcasting are intrenched. We may well continue with both the BBG and the CBC. It is the function of each element, and the nature of their relationships, that needs clear definition. We go back to the fundamental questions: What are the aims and purposes of broadcasting in Canada, and how can broadcasting best be organized to achieve these objectives?

When we have achieved a measure of national agreement on this question, then it will be possible to tackle the legion of issues that are plaguing broadcasting. For example:

— What should the role of the BBG be, and what should its proper relationship be to the CBC and to private television stations and networks?

— How can quality of programming *and* Canadian content best be achieved, and paid for?

— To what extent should the CBC engage in commercial broadcasting?

— What arrangements can be made for the financing of capital and operational expenditures on a regular basis, so that the CBC can make plans for its future development?

— How can the independent broadcasting stations and networks operate as successful private enterprises and still meet the responsibilities to the audience which are a condition of the granting of their licenses?

— What are the reasonable limits of radio and television service in Canada in terms of geography, language, hours of service, type of service (AM, FM, shortwave, TV— black and white and colour)?

— What control, if any, can or should be exercised in the case of the cable television and community antenna organisations? Each year an increasing number of Canadians use these services, which bring TV programs to their homes by cable and not through the airwaves, over which the BBG and the Department of Transport have authority.

II

THE BBG

II

THE BBG

The Board of Broadcast Governors, established by the Broadcasting Act, 1958, was first appointed November 10, 1958. It has three full-time members and 12 part-time members, for a total membership of 15.[1] The only member of the BBG with previous experience in broadcasting is the third full-time member, Bernard Goulet, who joined the BBG on January 1, 1961. He had been active in private broadcasting since 1938. The present staff of the BBG consists of 40 persons, including the three full-time members of the Board. Its budget covers mainly salaries, allowances and travel expenses.[2]

To replace the previous regulations, the BBG introduced new Broadcasting Regulations for television, on November 12, 1959, and there have been several amendments.[3] For

---

[1]On January 1, 1963, these members made up the Board of Broadcast Governors:

Full-time members:
    Chairman: Dr. Andrew Stewart
    Vice-Chairmen: Carlyle Allison
                      Bernard Goulet

Part-time members:
    Joseph F. Brown, Vancouver
    Mrs. Mabel G. Connell, Prince Albert
    Emlyn Davies, Toronto
    Claude B. Gagnon, Quebec City
    Edward A. Dunlop, Toronto
    Charles R. Chambers, Toronto
    Ivan Sabourin, Iberville
    Colin B. Mackay, Fredericton
    Roy D. Duchemin, Sydney
    Leslie M. Marshall, St. John's
    R. Louis Burge, St. Peters Bay
    John B. Lewis, Montreal

[2]Annual expenditures of the BBG:

To March 31, 1959 (part year)	$ 47,000.
1960	189,000.
1961	281,000.
1962	312,000.

[3]Dated March 13, 1961, March 10, 1962, May 9, 1962 and June 8, 1962.

17

radio, new regulations were introduced on November 22, 1961 as the Radio (AM) Broadcasting Regulations. Two amendments have been introduced, both dated March 10, 1962.

The Activities of the Board:

The BBG is the regulatory body for all broadcasting. Its responsibilities extend to public and private broadcasting, to television and to radio, both AM and FM.

The regulatory function was previously performed by the CBC. There was much criticism of this arrangement, chiefly from the private stations, on the grounds that the CBC was both referee and participant. It was admitted by the private stations that actually they got along well with the CBC. The objection was largely on theoretical grounds, and also on the basis that while they got along well with Mr. Davidson Dunton, who served as Chairman of the Board of Governors of the CBC from 1945 to 1958, a successor might be less amiable in his handling of disputes involving the private stations.

Critics of the performance of the private stations felt that the CBC was far too lenient. During the years when the regulation of all broadcasting was the responsibility of the CBC, no private station had its license revoked or suspended. In fact, no public warning was ever issued to a private station for failure to observe the regulations.

The Fowler Report expressed the opinion that the CBC had leaned over backwards in its dealings with the private stations.

The BBG is independent of the CBC and of the private stations. It is intended as an impartial regulating body for all broadcasting. It reports directly to Parliament, formerly through the Minister of National Revenue, and since August, 1962, through the Secretary of State.

The BBG is a regulatory body; the CBC an operating body. The conflicts between the two bodies spring largely from differences of opinion as to the manner and the extent to which the regulatory body, the BBG, can influence, directly or indirectly, the operations of the CBC. Underlying the differences which have caused friction between the two governing bodies is the absence of a clear statement in policy and legislation of the nature of Canada's broadcasting system.

The Fowler Report predicted that ". . . if the two bodies (as is probably more likely) pulled apart, one or other would be bound to assert dominance, through the skill and strength of personality of its members, especially of its chairman."

The two bodies have pulled apart, as predicted, but two strong-minded men are pitted against one another, and so far neither the CBC nor the BBG has emerged the dominant body. Alphonse Ouimet, an engineer by training, who has spent his life in broadcasting and with the CBC, has been the chief officer of the Corporation since the retirement of A. Davidson Dunton in 1958. Andrew Stewart, a former professor and university president has headed the BBG since it was established, at the end of 1958. Despite numerous meetings and informal discussions, a kind of stalemate has been reached, based partly on the fact that the Broadcasting Act of 1958 is a far from perfect piece of legislation, and partly on the fact that the basic premises of the CBC and the BBG differ, and consequently they interpret the legislation quite differently.

There have been three major disagreements, and one of these, the Grey Cup issue, was settled just short of the two bodies going to the courts to battle out their differing viewpoints. The other two disputes were the question of the second French television station license at Quebec City, and

the question of the right of a network affiliate to take programs from other networks (which was an intrinsic part of
the Grey Cup controversy).

The stalemate is likely to continue until the government
at Ottawa has reviewed the situation fully and responsibly
and has issued either a clarification of the Broadcasting Act
of 1958, or an entirely new piece of legislation which could
clarify the broadcasting situation for a period of years.

The battle over a third television license for Quebec City
led to the resignation of two members of the BBG, Dr.
Eugene A. Forsey, Ottawa, economist for the Canadian
Labour Congress, and Professor Guy Hudon, of Laval
University, Quebec.

There are two television stations in Quebec City, one
English and one French. Both stations are private, and there
is common ownership of the two stations. Each station is
affiliated with a CBC television network. The BBG decided
to hold hearings to decide the matter of a license for a third
television station in Quebec City. There were two applicants,
the CBC and a private applicant.

The private applicant was refused. Then, although it
had been agreed that the Quebec City area warranted a
second French television station, the majority of the BBG
members decided to postpone the decision on the CBC
application. At this point, the two members mentioned
above, resigned in protest. Their resignations were accepted
and they were later replaced on the Board. The reason given
for deferment was that the BBG wanted the CBC to supply
a complete report on its plans for future stations right across
Canada. The two members who resigned argued that this
was most unfair; that once the hearing was called, the Board
was under an obligation to make a decision and award a
license. Since the private application was refused, the other
application, that of the CBC, should have been awarded a
license. Only after a delay of several months did the BBG

decide to award to the CBC a license to operate a French language television station in Quebec City.

During the latter part of 1962, the three-way battle between the CBC, the CTV network and the BBG became a national issue. The argument concerned the Grey Cup match, the annual East-West football game to select the top professional team in the country. The dispute filled many columns on the sports page, and spread over to page one of the newspapers, and to the editorial pages. Several editorial page cartoons satirized the fact that the struggle over broadcasting rights was stealing the spotlight from the struggle between the two competing football clubs.

At one time the CBC carried the games and finals of the Canadian Football League on its national network. With the advent of a private TV network, there was suddenly sharp competition for the rights to broadcast these games. In April, 1962, bids were submitted by both the CBC and private television interests. The CBC bid for the right to televise the games on either a non-exclusive, or an exclusive basis. The rights were finally sold, for 1962, to the Toronto station, CFTO-TV, which purchased them on its own account, and on behalf of the CTV network, of which it is a member station.

The regular games of the season were broadcast over the stations of the private CTV network. The CTV network and CFTO-TV had asked the BBG to split the CBC network for football, but this request was refused. Apparently the sponsors were content with the coverage provided by CTV for the regular games. But, for the final game, they wanted full national coverage. The CBC was approached on the subject of the Grey Cup match, by CTV and CFTO-TV. Here a difference of opinion exists about a letter on this subject written by Mr. John Bassett, chief executive officer and one of the principal owners of CFTO-TV. Mr. Bassett is also publisher of the daily newspaper, the Toronto *Telegram*.

The CBC interpreted Mr. Bassett's letter to contain an offer to provide the CBC with the broadcast of the Grey Cup match on an unsponsored basis, if they did not wish to accept it with commercials. The private television group interpreted the letter to mean that the CBC could have the broadcast on an unsponsored basis, only if they could not reach a satisfactory financial arrangement with the sponsors.

The sponsors were quite willing to pay the CBC to carry the Grey Cup match over the national TV English network. It will be remembered that most of the stations that compose the CBC national network are privately-owned television stations. They have agreements with the CBC, covering their affiliation with the CBC network. The CBC was battling for a principle. It did not want any outside party, either the rival CTV network, or the BBG, to be in a position to tell the CBC that the Corporation must broadcast a particular programme, complete with commercials. The CBC was at all times ready to carry the Grey Cup match, but it insisted on its right to carry the programme without commercial announcements, even though this meant the loss of some $41,000 in revenue to the CBC and its member stations.

The battle raged back and forth; no attempt will be made here to list all the meetings, the correspondence, the long distance telephone calls, the telegrams that shot back and forth between the various parties involved. The commercial sponsors were very much involved in the dispute, as were their advertising agencies.

The BBG expressed the view that the Grey Cup match was an event of interest to Canadians in all parts of the country. The BBG announced that it would pass a regulation requiring the CBC to carry the Grey Cup match, complete with commercial announcements.

The Grey Cup controversy raged all during the summer of 1962. On August 18, a public hearing was held in Ottawa. The various parties to the dispute expressed their views.

The gloves were off. The CBC stated that it had consulted the Attorney General's department, which expressed the opinion that the BBG regulation was illegal. The CBC was prepared to take the matter to the courts. The private broadcasters, including in their ranks some former long-time employees of the CBC, were bitter in their attacks on the Corporation. The CBC was represented as preventing Canadians from enjoying a sporting event of utmost interest to the nation.

The CBC stuck to its guns. Despite the arguments of the private telecasters that it was physically impossible to provide the CBC with a "clean-feed"—a broadcast free of any commercial messages—that is what finally happened. In a frantic, last-minute effort, agreement was reached between the CBC and the individual advertisers that the CBC would carry the telecast, and would provide courtesy announcements to the sponsors, to thank them for their cooperation in making the programme available to the audience of the CBC national network. But, the regular commercial announcements would not be carried. The CBC would carry the programme as a public service; neither the CBC nor its members would receive any advertising revenue.

The BBG regulation compelling the CBC to carry the football game and the commercials, announced on November 7, was never enforced. When the courtesy announcement arrangement was worked out between the CBC and the advertisers, the BBG accepted this as a workable compromise.

The point at issue, control over the CBC network and the relations between the CBC and the private stations that are members of this network, has yet to be finally settled.

The BBG has made a number of attempts to loosen the CBC's hold on its network affiliates. A so-called "Cross-Programming" regulation was introduced which would have enabled CBC affiliate stations to make other network arrangements at times when they were not committed to the CBC network. The CBC objected that this threatened the entire network structure which is the basis of a national service in television. The CBC argued that, according to the terms of the Broadcasting Act of 1958, the BBG could not permit an affiliate to make such arrangements without the consent of the network operator. Following a full discussion by the Board of Broadcast Governors, the "cross-programming" regulation was reversed on June 20, 1961. The Grey Cup controversy presented the same issue, in another guise. As matters now stand, both Canadian television networks, the CBC and the CTV, have the right to decide whether any individual station member can establish a temporary link with another network. Officials of CTV argue that when their members ask permission to join the CBC network for a particular programme, they are given this permission without question.

The BBG would like the government to indicate whether or not it supports the point of view expressed by Mr. Ouimet, president of the CBC, when he urges that the CBC should own and operate its own television stations at key points from coast to coast. This would mean that the national television service would no longer be dependent on private television stations to ensure national coverage. Once the CBC had its own facilities, private stations which are now members of the CBC network, and have network agreements with the CBC, would be free to join the private television network, or operate independently, as they saw fit.

The BBG argues that if the policy of the government is to provide the CBC with its own transmitting facilities across Canada, then there is no point in holding public hearings to consider competitive bids for TV licenses in certain locations, where it is government policy to allow the CBC to establish its own facilities. Where there is only one frequency available, or where the area can only support one station, or one additional station, then a private applicant would be put to needless expense if he were to make application for a license at a location that was essential to the CBC for national coverage. Preparing an application for a private television license can involve an expenditure of $30,000. to $50,000. on the part of the applicant.

This is typical of the problems created by the lack of a clear policy on the role which broadcasting should play in our society.

Representatives of both the BBG and the CBC have expressed the view that there are certain important areas of difference between them, whch they cannot settle between themselves. They would like a decision to be made by the body that is senior to both of them, Parliament.

The BBG recognizes that the CBC has certain special responsibilities, but it would like these spelt out more clearly by Parliament. Aside from this, it sees it as its duty to treat private and public broadcasters with equal fairness and justice.

The growing discord between the BBG and the CBC is in contrast to the good relations which exist between the private television stations, the CTV network and the BBG. It was government policy to establish second TV stations in main centres, once the national TV service of the CBC was established. It should be noted, however, that the CBC owns and operates only 14 manned television stations. The rest of the extensive television network coverage of the CBC is provided by 47 privately-owned television stations which have affiliation agreements with the CBC.

Once the CBC television network was established, second television stations were licensed to private operators in eight major centres of population. Because of the high cost of providing television programs, the idea of a private TV network was soon being discussed. The decision to license a private television network was taken on the initiative of the

BBG; the BBG has the power to do this, but it did not have a specific instruction from Parliament to do so. A license was granted to a private network, CTV Television Network Ltd. in 1961. Some observers consider that the step was premature. However, CTV is now a going concern. It is known that at the outset some of the stations, which are now affiliates, objected to the original form of CTV. As affiliates they now own some 20 per cent of the shares in the network, and as part-owners they are naturally involved in, and concerned for, its well being.

It is sometimes said that the events since the appearance of the BBG give support to the allegation that the BBG favours the private broadcasters. Members of the BBG have all been appointed by a Conservative government that has not been friendly to the CBC, although members of the party have at times conceded the importance of a national service in broadcasting, free from political influence.

It has been argued that the key officials of the CBC may be responsible in part for the differences with the BBG. The BBG took over the regulatory function in broadcasting, and there can be no question that by law it is the senior body in broadcasting. Since this position previously was occupied by the CBC for many years, it is possible that some permanent CBC officials have been reluctant to accept the authority of men who have only recently arrived on the broadcasting scene, and lack the long years of experience of certain CBC executives.

There are some very human elements in the problem. While the BBG is not at all the kind of body recommended by *The Fowler Report*, it is possible that broadcasting could get along with two Boards, a BBG and a Board of Directors of the CBC. But, it would require a great effort on the part of the "old-timers" to accept the "newcomers" without resentment.

It should be noted that the members appointed to the CBC Board of Directors were also nominated by a Conservative government, and were also completely new to the field of broadcasting. Yet, they quickly became staunch defenders of the rights and responsibilities of the national broadcasting service.

It has been suggested that several members of the BBG were critical in print of the CBC before being appointed to their present positions. It is possible that the difficulties with the CBC are helping to drive the members of the BBG into the arms of the private television stations and the CTV network.

The Parliamentary Committee report of 1961 contained none of the usual complimentary remarks on the work of the CBC which has been part of parliamentary reports on broadcasting during both Liberal and Conservative governments in the past.

The members of the BBG argue that they are merely following the directions contained in the Broadcasting Act of 1958. If the government had clearly indicated that it intended to curtail the CBC's activities, all concerned would know where they stand. But, for the most part the view that the CBC is in official disfavour has been a matter of rumour, rather than of record.

III

THE CBC

THE CBC

The Canadian Broadcasting Corporation was established in 1936. It inherited from its predecessor, the Canadian Radio Broadcasting Commission, a staff of 130 persons and seven low power stations. At that time, radio reached about 50 per cent of the population.

In the years that followed, radio broadcasting grew rapidly in Canada. Television, which began in 1952, experienced a wildfire growth. Counting unmanned rebroadcasting and relay stations, there are today some 541 broadcasting transmitters in Canada: AM, FM and short-wave radio and television. Of these, 356 transmitters, both CBC and private, serve as outlets for the national services provided by the CBC in French and English, by radio and by television. In 1962, the Corporation had some 8,000 employees. Of the homes in Canada, 89 per cent have television and 96 per cent have radio.

Of 48 stations connected with the CBC English television network; 10 are owned by the CBC and 38 are privately owned. Of 13 stations connected with the CBC French television network, 4 are owned by the CBC and 9 are privately owned.

In AM radio, the CBC English network has a total of 78 stations of which 24 are owned by the CBC and 54 are privately owned. The CBC French radio network has a total of 30 stations; of these 4 are owned by the CBC, 26 are privately owned.[1]

These figures give a clear indication of the extent to which the CBC depends on its affiliation arrangements with private stations to secure national coverage in both radio and television.

---

[1]As of March 12, 1963. Figures are from the "Fact Sheet" prepared by the CBC in consultation with the BBG and the Department of Transport.

Particularly since the advent of television, the CBC has become a large-scale institution with a Board of Directors of eleven.[2] Its annual budget is more than $100 millions. It has grown a long way from the radio days when its financial needs could be met out of a one dollar radio license fee, which later grew to two dollars, to be finally abolished in 1953.

An excise tax on radio and television sets and parts still provides revenue which the Fowler Report indicated should be sufficient to meet the CBC's capital requirements. But, the Fowler Report foresaw that in future years the CBC would require large sums of money, in addition to its commercial revenue, to meet its operating expenditures.

The only source available for these funds is Parliament. In 1962 approximately one-third of the CBC's revenue came from advertising; two-thirds came from public funds.

While the sums involved are large, comparison with sums spent on broadcasting in countries with a comparable level of service would indicate that Canadian expenditures on a per capita basis are not out of line. However, some Canadians continue to argue that we should take our example from the United States, where radio and television are provided "free", without any cost to the taxpayer.

As one by-product of its rapid growth, the physical facilities of the CBC in Ottawa, Toronto and Montreal are scattered, resulting in inconvenience and expense. The

---

[2]The Board of Directors of the CBC includes (January 1, 1963) :

J. A. Ouimet, Ottawa, (President)
W. E. S. Briggs, Ottawa, (Vice-President)
R. L. Dunsmore, Montreal, (Chairman)
C. B. Lumsden, Wolfville, N.S., (Vice-Chairman)
Mrs. Ellen Armstrong, Calgary
N. B. Buchanan, St. Stephen, N.B.
Mrs. Alice Carter, Salmon Arm, B.C.
Raymond Dupuis, Montreal
Frederick L. Jenkins, London, Ont.
W. L. Morton, Winnipeg
Roger N. Séguin, Q.C., Ottawa

Corporation now intends to consolidate its operations in these three centres. Plans are underway to build a $3 million Ottawa headquarters. It will be a six-storey building with three wings and will be constructed on a 15 acre plot of land. It will house CBC head office staff now accommodated in eight separate locations.

A footnote to the CBC financial statement in its Annual Report for 1961-1962 reads as follows:

Proposed Consolidation of Facilities in Toronto, Montreal and Ottawa. Capital assets shown above in the amount of $55,890,783 includes the sum of $1,869,000 expended during the last three years in connection with proposed consolidation of facilities in Toronto, Montreal and Ottawa. It is estimated that the total cost of consolidation of facilities at these locations will be $81,087,000. of which, subject to the provision by Parliament of annual appropriations for the purpose, approximately $2,890,000 will be expended during the year ending March 31, 1963 and $76,328,000 during the three years ending March 31, 1966.

This item is reproduced here, because it underlines one of the main problems of the CBC: the difficulty of operating a major national institution, and of making plans for future growth and development, without any clear assurance that it has general approval from Parliament for its plans, and with no assurance that the money necessary for capital and operational purposes will be available. The government's austerity program in 1962 did, in fact, delay these consolidation plans, as well as other planned activities of the Corporation.

The Fowler Commission was never in any doubt about the role of the CBC. This had been made clear by the Government, in appointing the Royal Commission: "It was a condition and basic assumption of the inquiry that the broadcasting and distribution of Canadian programs by a public agency shall continue to be the central feature of Canadian broadcasting policy."

The Fowler Report also recognized the financial realities involved in such a policy.

If we are to have a Canadian broadcasting system, with some flow of programs in an east-west direction across the country, with some Canadian content and with some contribution to a Canadian national consciousness, there must be a public broadcasting agency supported by substantial amounts of public money.

The Fowler Commission was also keenly aware of the fact which has been referred to in this study as the basic issue: that while there is indecision about the form of the Canadian system of broadcasting it is impossible for broadcasters—both public and private—to get on with their job of producing programs for Canadians. There is a hope expressed in *The Fowler Report* of 1957 that is still not realized:

It may be that when our considerations have been considered, and adopted or rejected, the true nature of our broadcasting system can be clarified, and further debate can be directed towards the operation of the system rather than on repetitious arguments concerning the basis of the system.

The Fowler Report stated that the CBC must have its task clearly defined, that it must operate efficiently, and that it must have assured financial support to carry out its assigned task. In the words of the *Report*:

The Canadian Broadcasting Corporation, as the public operating agency in the Canadian broadcasting system, should have its task clearly defined, should know the limits beyond which it is not expected to go, and should have the means and the power to discharge that task within those limits.

In general, *The Fowler Report* spoke well of the CBC and its efforts. It was critical of the programming of CJBC, Toronto, the basic station of the CBC's Dominion Network.

It rated CJBC as no better than some of the worst of the commercial stations. It criticized the CBC for failing to publicize its own efforts. It urged the CBC to compete more vigorously for commercial revenue.

It took the CBC five years to get around to liquidating the Dominion Network, in a consolidation step in mid-1962. The CBC has been more active in recent years in publicizing its own efforts on its own programs, and in paid advertisements and releases which appear in the press. It has been very vigorous in pursuing commercial revenue, to the extent that some people within the CBC feel that the Corporation is losing its soul, while outside critics suggest that the CBC program schedule is getting to look more and more like that of its American and Canadian rivals. Certainly the private television stations and the new CTV network are not happy about the $33 millions in commercial revenues which the CBC pocketed in 1962.

Present BBG regulations require that Canadian television stations and networks offer 55 per cent Canadian content. (They require only 45 per cent during the summer months.) The *Winnipeg Tribune* devoted its entire editorial page on November 24, 1962, to an effort to interpret the term (with some help from the BBG) and came up with some curious results:

— The World Series.
  Complete Canadian content credit under Section 6 (4) e of Canadian content regulations.

— President Kennedy addressing the U.S. nation.
  Wholly Canadian content.

— A Brigitte Bardot movie made in France.
  Qualifies under Section 6 (5) b as 50 per cent Canadian in its French language version. In English, it would rate as foreign.

— Romper Room.

When produced in Canada by a Canadian station is considered wholly Canadian. No penalty is exacted because the script is written in the United States, however much the Board might prefer to see such programs written as well as produced in Canada by Canadians.

— Ivanhoe.

A Commonwealth production and accorded appropriate Canadian content.

The CBC English television network claims that some 65 per cent of its content is Canadian, produced by the CBC. About 30 per cent of the network's program content comes from the United States. The CBC French television network has a better record, claiming more than 75 per cent of original Canadian programs, and 12 per cent of its programs from the United States.

The record of CBC radio, English and French, shows much less U.S. influence: only three per cent of programs come from the United States.

Since 1952 the advertiser has shifted much of his attention from radio to television. Before the appearance of television, the important revenue producers in broadcasting were the network radio programs. With the rise of television, commercial radio network programs almost ceased to exist. Radio stations as a group have maintained their share of advertising revenue, and have even shown small increases. Today, however, the local radio station depends chiefly on the local advertiser and on spot advertising placed by national advertisers. Also, there are many more radio stations in operation today to share the radio advertising dollars. The revenues of a few radio stations have increased, but many more radio stations are just holding their own, and some radio stations have actually seen their revenues decline since the advent of television.

Today it is network television that attracts the national advertisers with large sums of money to spend. This was unquestionably a factor in the establishment of the private television network.

Estimates for 1960 indicate that 96.8 per cent of *radio* advertising revenue went to 193 private stations, and the balance, 3.2 per cent, went to the CBC.

In television, estimates for the same year, 1960, indicate that 65 per cent of *television* advertising revenue went to the private TV stations, and 35 per cent went to the CBC. With the revenues of network television mounting steadily and rapidly, it hardly comes as a surprise to learn that the private television network operators would like the CBC to withdraw from all commercial activity, leaving them to pick up the slice of TV commercial revenue which the CBC now earns.

It is equally obvious that there is no money of any significance to be earned in network radio. Private broadcasters showed no interest in the suggestion that a private national radio network be formed. The private stations are glad to leave the CBC with the responsibilities for a national radio network, which offers little opportunity for commercial revenue.

The CBC has never been short of critics. Today, critics are to be found even among the ranks of those who consider themselves friends of the CBC, and among CBC employees. The current criticisms heard most frequently are:

(1) That the organization is inefficient; while there are many capable and diligent employees, there are also many who do not earn their pay. In particular, the organization is criticized for being top-heavy with executives. (2) In the matter of programming, the Corporation is considered to be lacking in the kind of lively, imaginative broadcasting that in past years earned it a shining reputation at home and abroad. (3) That the CBC has gone too commercial.

It is possible that there is a relationship between the first two criticisms. With the rapid growth of the CBC, and with the expansion of the staff located in Ottawa, there may have come a tendency to consider administration more important than programming. Perhaps it is necessary to remind the CBC now and then that the acid test of its operations is at all times the quality of programs that it offers. The job of the executive is to back up, support, encourage and assist the program producer in his efforts. The greater the number of executives that have to approve any program project, the greater the possibility that concern with criticism from Parliament, or from newspaper critics of the CBC, will weaken the hand of the producer.

In a major test of morale in 1959, the CBC came through with its colours flying. The issue involved the program "Preview Commentary". Rather than yield to political pressure, the three top men in charge of the Public Affairs Department—Frank Peers, Hugh Gillis and Bernard Trotter —submitted their resignations. Immediately, almost every producer and organizer of Public Affairs programs from coast to coast followed their example. The Board of Directors of the CBC asked the management of the CBC not to accept these resignations. After appearing before the 1959 Parliamentary Committee on Broadcasting, the top executives of the Public Affairs Department agreed to the request to withdraw their resignations, and they and their associates returned to work. The incident demonstrated that there were men and women in the CBC who understood that without autonomy in the planning and preparation of programs, and without freedom from interference by the government of the day, the CBC was not worth its salt.

It is possible that the CBC is no more executive-ridden, and no more lacking in nerve than any private corporation of the same size. But, the CBC does live in a glass house. It is exposed to the strong light of criticism from every side.

Private corporations are perhaps better able to conceal their mistakes and to treat the lack of an adventuresome spirit as prudent conservatism.

A study of the CBC television schedule for a typical week reveals that on many evenings, during the peak viewing hours between 7:30 p.m. and 10 p.m., the time devoted to network and film programs from the United States far outbalances the time devoted to Canadian programs. Obviously, these are the most saleable hours. But, is the CBC performing its function as a national service if it weights the balance heavily in favour of imported TV programs during those hours when most Canadians choose to watch television?

One of the ways in which the CBC presents its own story, attractively and forthrightly, is in its annual report. In the annual report for 1961-1962, R. L. Dunsmore, Chairman of the Board of Directors, indicates clearly the Corporation's views on the two contentious questions of cross-programming and disaffiliation. Dunsmore asks:

"That the procedure laid down in the Broadcasting Act whereby approval of the parent network be secured by licensees of broadcasting stations before operating as part of another network be adhered to."

"That whenever it is necessary to maintain adequate distribution of the national service, the Corporation shall oppose applications for disaffiliation from any CBC affiliated stations."

The President of the CBC, Alphonse Ouimet, argues the case even more directly: "CTV, the second network, has said that is requires more outlets. During the past year the CBC has said emphatically that it would not split its networks. Our stand on this matter of vital public interest remains unchanged."

The President also took the occasion to state: "The CBC believes that a major study of broadcasting in Canada should be carried out periodically to resolve any expressed or un-expressed doubts which inevitably develop as previous findings fade with time."

Finally, Mr. Ouimet closes his section of the report "by reiterating the aims of the national broadcasting service". He proceeds to list what he considers the four basic principles which comprise the CBC's mandate from Parliament.

1. *To be a complete service,* covering in fair proportion the whole range of programming; bringing things of interest, value, and entertainment to people of all tastes, ages and interests, and not concentrating on some aspects of broadcasting to the exclusion of others.

2. *To link all parts of the country* in two ways:
     (1) through the inclusion of a wide variety of national and common interests in its program services;
     (2) by using its physical resources to bring the national program service to as many Canadians as finances allow. Whether Canadians live in remote or heavily-populated areas the national system should serve them as adequately and equitably as possible.

3. *To be predominantly Canadian in content and character.* It should serve Canadian needs and bring Canadians in widely-separated parts of the country closer together, contributing to the development and preservation of a sense of national unity.

4. *To serve equitably* the two main language groups and cultures, and the special needs of Canada's various geographical regions.

By contrast, the annual reports of the BBG are arid factual accounts. It might be useful if the BBG were to make use of its annual reports to present to the Canadian public and to Parliament its understanding of the nature of broadcasting, and its suggestions for changes needed to make the broadcasting system operate more effectively.

At the highest levels, within the CBC, differences about CBC policies are encountered. In its barest form, the main difference can be defined as a battle of programming versus operations.

The program group consider that the emphasis on commercialism and on physical resources is too often at the expense of the essential responsibility of the CBC to present a well-balanced, high quality schedule of Canadian programs for Canadians. Concern with administrative matters in the large and growing Corporation, plus emphasis on extending physical facilities, tends to rate the program producer second to the administrator and the engineer.

The people who emphasize the program responsibilities of the CBC do not consider that the CBC should drop all commercial broadcasts. The CBC should continue to carry certain commercial broadcasts, but the number and distribution of such programs should be better balanced than at present.

Physical facilities for better coverage are important. But, what is the purpose of reaching every last Canadian with a radio and television signal, if you do not have an attractive variety of interesting and informative Canadian programs to offer?

Should the CBC drop all commercials? This would by no means guarantee a better variety and quality of Canadian programming. The commercial revenue which the CBC earns is highly useful to the Corporation; it reduces the amount that must be sought from Parliament each year. It is possible that the CBC can provide an interesting schedule of Canadian programs, some sponsored and some unsponsored, without losing its soul. Certainly, there is greater danger in the suggestion that all commercial programs be handled by the private stations, and all non-commercial programs by the CBC. The almost inevitable result would be a pressure to unload all the heavy and serious programs on to the CBC, leaving the private stations and networks to handle all the light, variety entertainment. This is the surest way to split the audience in two, and create a split in the population between those who want serious fare, and those who want light fare. It is also a device for shifting the responsibility for providing Canadian programs and making use of Canadian talent onto the CBC. Such a division of programs between the CBC and the private broadcasters would permit the latter to concentrate on mass audiences and profits, regardless of whether or not they provide proper balance in their program schedules.

Revenue from advertising provides an important part of the budget of the CBC. Nevertheless, its first responsibility and purpose remains: to provide a national broadcasting service of excellence.

IV

RADIO CANADA

RADIO CANADA

The title Canadian Broadcasting Corporation, or *Radio Canada* in French, covers the total operation of the CBC. We are here examining briefly the French side of the national broadcasting service. One face of the Corporation, the CBC, speaks English; the other face known as *Radio Canada*, speaks French. While the two faces are both part of the same organization, they rarely look at one another. It would be a step towards greater understanding between the English and the French in Canada, if there were more exchanges between them.

The centre of French language broadcasting is the *Radio Canada* building in downtown Montreal. Here the Quebec region of the Corporation has its headquarters. From the 12-storey building, programs go out in French over a radio network that reaches eight of the 10 provinces, with Newfoundland and British Columbia the only exceptions. The French TV network extends from Moncton to Winnipeg.

According to *Radio Canada* publicist Paul Sabourin, writing in the *Canadian Broadcaster,* the Montreal centre is the world's largest producer of French language programs, exceeding the output of France's *Radiodiffusion-Télévision Française* (RTF). Sabourin rates Montreal as the third television production centre in the world, after New York and Hollywood.

The radio network of *Radio Canada* links 30 stations, four of which are owned by the government body; the remainder are private affiliates. French language television links 13 stations, four of which are owned by *Radio Canada*. In addition, French programs are distributed by video tape and film to six English language television stations in Ontario and Western Canada.

The 1961 census reported the population of Quebec province at 5,259,211. Nine out of ten inhabitants of the

45

province are of French origin. It is true that in Montreal many people of French origin speak English, but in other centres, such as Quebec City, the capital of the province, and in the rural areas of Quebec, more than 9 out of 10 inhabitants speak only French.

Outside the province of Quebec there are pockets of French population ranging from the numerous Acadians of New Brunswick who recently helped to elect a premier of French origin, to isolated groups of French in British Columbia.

Radio Canada began with an unique advantage. The barrier of language tends to shield its audience from the competition of United States broadcasters. Programs were exchanged with France, Belgium and other French language countries, but not to anything like the extent that CBC English television was dependent on programs imported from the United States. It was the language barrier that placed great emphasis on live production, and made Montreal one of the leading centres in the world for the production of live programs. But, this initial advantage is being whittled away. Many United States TV series are being "dubbed", mostly in Paris, some of them in Montreal, and they are turning up with greater frequency on the program schedules of *Radio Canada*.

Despite this trend, Montreal is still a lively production centre. More than 2,500 people are employed at *Radio Canada* headquarters in Montreal, most of them busy with programs in the French language. The *Radio Canada* operation employs more than 100 TV producers and some 40 radio producers. To accommodate this activity, *Radio Canada* has eight television studios and three mobile TV units, plus 21 radio studios. The radio studios also serve the International Service and the Northern Service of the CBC and the same building serves as the centre for English radio and television activities in the province of Quebec.

In the field of the arts and information, *Radio Canada* has distinguished itself with such programs as *L'heure du concert* which has brought outstanding ballet, opera and concert music to English as well as French audiences. Plays by such masters as Racine, Ben Jonson and Chekhov have been staged on its program, *télétheatre,* along with the works of leading French-Canadian playwrights. The program, *Point de mir,* offered provocative lectures on current affairs by René Levesque, but it disappeared from the air even before Mr. Levesque left to take a direct hand in politics as Minister of Natural Resources for Quebec. One of the current public affairs programs is *Premier plan* (it has its counterpart in *Close-Up* on the English network) which roves the world exploring topics and personalities in depth. For children, *Radio Canada* presents *Le grand duc* which dramatizes tales and legends of Canada and other countries for youngsters. *La vie qui bat* offers stories of animal life. Children come into direct touch with television through *Caravane,* a show for children which travels about to various parts of Quebec.

Radio Canada has developed a number of popular French Canadian broadcasts, which attract wide audiences. The skill of French writers and actors has made the *"téléroman"* and the *"radioroman"* part of the French Canadian tradition. These are daily serialized programs, one of which, Claude-Henri Grignon's *Un homme et son péché* (A Man and His Sin), has been popular on radio for 24 years. The television version of the same program has been running for seven years. The program is set in the Laurentian area of Quebec during the 1880's and the characters are probably better known to their audience than their next door neighbours. The variety radio show, *Les Joyeux Troubadors* has been on the air for 23 years. A popular breakfast time show with the French radio audience, *Chez Miville,* has been running for eight years.

The leading French programs attract very substantial audiences. Audiences of from two to three million persons are not uncommon for such popular TV programs as *La poule aux oeufs d'or* (a contest program, The Hen That Lays the Golden Eggs), *Music-Hall,* and major league hockey.

A limited market abroad has been found for some of *Radio Canada's* productions. The most significant trade is with France. For several years, *Radio Canada* has had its own representative in Paris. During 1963, a full-time representative of the French RTF will take up his duties in Montreal to facilitate the exchange of programs between Paris and Montreal.

The French language has not proved an invulnerable barrier. On the French networks of *Radio Canada* one will find an increasing number of U.S. programs such as *Father Knows Best* "dubbed" into French in Paris and disguised as *Papa a raison,* and *Robin Hood,* dubbed in Montreal and posing as *Robin des bois.* Because many of these programs have already covered their costs in the United States, they can be dumped on the Canadian market and other French-language markets at very low prices, certainly far below the cost of live production.

Radio Canada helps to bring together most of the French speaking population of Canada. An interesting chapter in the story of French language broadcasting began in the 1940's when a number of French speaking residents of the Prairie provinces got together to discuss the use of broadcasting to serve and preserve their culture. The result was the establishment at St. Boniface, Manitoba, of a company to operate a French language radio station. The station, CKSB, went on the air in 1946. Today, this private, commercial station broadcasts with 10,000 watts of power and is reported to be doing quite well financially, although the primary motive of the founders who put up the capital to establish the station was to maintain the French culture in Western Canada. In 1949, a French station, CHFA, was established at Edmonton. In 1952, two French stations were set up in Saskatchewan, CFNS at Saskatoon and CFRO in Gravelbourg. In the same year, 1952, all four French Prairie stations were linked for the first time with the *Radio Canada* network.

Broadcasting in the French language in Canada is a lively enterprise. In the course of serving the audience with a high proportion of Canadian programs, many of them live, *Radio Canada* also plays the role of a patron of the arts and of the artists. *Radio Canada* provides considerable employment for writers, producers, actors, artists and musicians. Many creative people living in Montreal earn a good living from broadcasting. Some Quebec artists and entertainers have gone to work in the entertainment centres of France and of the United States. But there is less pressure and less necessity to leave the country than with Canada's English speaking artists.

The private broadcasters, French as well as English, contribute very little to the employment of Canadian talent. Many of the stations, particularly in the main cities, are extremely profitable. Yet only from 1 to 2 per cent of their revenue goes for talent other than disk jockeys and news announcers. It has been estimated that some of the leading radio stations could provide an additional 30 hours per week of live programming, and still show a profit.

During the regime of Duplessis, *Radio Canada* was hampered in its efforts at educational broadcasting. Now it is moving into this field. With the cooperation and encouragement of the Lesage government a series of school programs was begun in February, 1963. Even before that date a start had been made with the broadcasting of credit courses from the University of Montreal.

If English speaking Canadians know little about the exciting programs and personalities that originate in Montreal, the fault may be partly their own, but it is also partly the fault of the parent Canadian Broadcasting Corporation. The job of helping French and English Canadians to understand each other better is being carried out with rather less success than some other responsibilities of the Corporation. In a survey released by CBC in April, 1963, some 30 percent of English Canadians expressed dissatisfaction on this score, and a somewhat smaller proportion of French Canadians were critical of the job that is being done to achieve better relations between the two main language groups.

Writing in the magazine *Canadian Art*,[1] Neil Morrison, former Supervisor of Public Affairs for the CBC, had this to say: "In effect, CBC and *Radio Canada* are two separate and almost independently run TV networks which nevertheless maintain friendly, even cordial diplomatic and cooperative relationships. But mutual planning and joint use of common program material is relatively limited."

Better understanding, plus a rich new source of talent, entertainment and information may become available to Canadians when CBC and *Radio Canada* move several steps further in the direction of mutual exchange.

---

[1]September-October 1962.

V

THE PRIVATE BROADCASTERS

THE PRIVATE BROADCASTERS

In March 1963 there were in operation in Canada a total of 245 private radio stations and 60 private television stations. A majority of the private television stations are linked with the national service as affiliates or supplementary stations of the networks operated by the CBC. But, in radio, 2 out of 3 private stations are completely outside the sphere of the CBC's national radio service.

The time-honoured view that in Canada we have a single broadcasting system made up of private and public elements, is in need of serious re-examination. If this view of Canadian broadcasting was ever true, it is much less true at the present time, and is becoming even less true with each new broadcasting license that is issued.

On the positive side, the private broadcasters have a continuous history dating back to 1920, the very dawn of broadcasting in Canada. Private broadcasters have invested considerable private capital in studios and broadcasting equipment. Without these investments, either the government would have had to appropriate much greater sums of money to provide broadcasting facilities, or many areas of Canada would have been deprived of broadcasting services.

The local private broadcasting station renders an important communication service to the community. In addition to providing news and music, it publicizes local activities by churches, fraternal organizations and charities. It affords local employment to a certain number of persons such as engineers, announcers, salesmen and office workers.

For the local merchant and the national advertiser, radio and television provide effective alternative methods of telling their advertising story, in addition to the daily and weekly newspapers, magazines, billboards and other media.

As in every form of human activity, there are good broadcasters and bad broadcasters. The number of good broadcasters in Canada is not large, but their names are well

known in the broadcasting community. They are the operators of the stations who regard broadcasting as something
more than a business. They take seriously the obligation to
perform a public service, which is clearly spelled out in the
granting of a license. These stations employ well-qualified
personnel. They draw on whatever talent is available in the
community, employ it, encourage its development. Instead
of putting all profits into the bank, they devote a portion of
their income to employing local musicians, writers and
singers for the production of live, Canadian broadcasts.

The vast majority of broadcasters do a job that can be
most charitably described as adequate. They perform a
service just sufficient to meet the minimum requirements of
the broadcasting license. They employ a small, over-worked
staff that is neither too well paid nor too well qualified. For
broadcast material they depend almost entirely on the wire
services for news, on recordings for radio, and film in cans
for television. Their main concern is to sell sufficient advertising to meet their costs of operation and show a profit
to the owner. Many serve communities with a limited economic potential, and they do the best job they can with the
limited revenue available to them.

A minority of broadcasters, as in any profession or line
of human endeavour, bring discredit to the entire group by
their shabby performances. These are the broadcasters who
hold a low view of public taste, and who will argue that by
achieving a high audience rating—regardless of the methods
used—they are catering to the real needs and demands of the
audience. In this category are the rock-and-roll stations
which feature the tense, frenetic type of announcer who has
nothing intelligent to say but tries to make every word he
breathes sound like a momentous and exciting pronounce-
ment.

These are the broadcasters known colloquially as "fast-
buck" operators, who often build up the revenues of a station and then sell and get out of town. The quiz program

with lucrative prizes for a nonsensical contest is a characteristic device of the broadcaster who feels no sense of community service or responsibility for the public franchise which he has been granted.

For him, the license is a valuable asset for which he pulled many strings, and may even have gambled some of his own cash, to obtain. He will promise the licensing authorities anything, and deliver as little as he feels he can get away with. His entire objective is to maximise his audience, thus providing the high ratings which will convince the advertisers that they are "buying" a very large number of listeners or viewers per dollar. This assures him of plenty of advertising revenue. Then, by keeping salaries and expenses to a minimum, and spending practically nothing on local talent and live shows, he can be assured of a fat annual income. The number of such broadcasters is few. They tend to flourish in the major cities, where large audiences and substantial advertising revenues can be achieved quickly by cynical operators who treat the audience as a chattel, to be bought and sold. The names of such broadcasters are well known in broadcasting circles. A few of their colleagues may envy them their financial success, but most broadcasters strongly resent the damage which their venality and lack of responsibility does to the private broadcasters as a group.

In 1960, the private broadcasting industry showed a net income of $9.9 million. While some stations earn substantial profits, others are small operations that show little profit, or lose money.

Dr. John A. Dawson, Director of Research for the BBG, in a paper on "The Economics of Broadcasting" read to the Canadian Political Science Association in June, 1962, reported:

Many of the units are small; for example, in 1960, out of 193 private radio stations for which the D.B.S. report contained information, 57 were in a revenue group with less than $100,000 revenue, and a further 73 received from $100,000 to $200,000. There were 6 with revenue of $1 million or over. Of 47 private television stations, 10 received less than $200,000 and a further 24 between $200,000 and $600,000. There were 7 with revenue of $1 million or over.

The 57 radio stations with less than $100,000 revenue per station reported aggregate revenue less than their aggregate expenses. Expenses were also greater than revenue for the 10 television stations with revenue of less than $200,000 per station. Some of these would be new stations losing money in the early years of getting established. While it is possible for some radio and television stations to show substantial profits, mainly in the largest cities, a number of stations in smaller centres must be satisfied with small profits, or may even operate at a loss.

Dr. Dawson points out that in broadcasting the consumer does not pay directly for the main product, the program. This is paid for by the advertiser, entirely in the case of private broadcasting, and partially in the case of the CBC. "It is apparent that we cannot expect from private broadcasters all of the things that Canadians wish to obtain from broadcasting. The incentives under which they operate press them to be at least partially concerned with service to advertisers."

The advocates of private broadcasting sometimes claim that while the national service of the CBC costs the taxpayers millions of dollars annually, private broadcasting provides programs "free". The classic argument is that mass advertising makes possible mass production, which lowers the cost of goods to the consumer. But it must be recognized that whether the payment for the cost of broadcasts is made through tax contributions, or is a part of the price of the goods which the consumer buys, it is the public that ultimately must provide the funds for all broadcasting, public and private.

Several facts have been clearly established about the licenses that are issued to private broadcasters by the Department of Transport, on the advice of the BBG. The would-be broadcaster must apply for the license and must indicate his ability to provide broadcasting service under the conditions and subject to the regulations of the Broadcasting Act. The licensee has no property right in the frequency which he is allowed to use. The license must be applied for anew, and must be issued anew at least every five years. The Broadcasting Act provides for a maximum penalty of three months suspension of license for failing to comply with the conditions of the license. The licensee may appeal the decision to the Exchequer Court of Canada, on points of law.

The private broadcaster looks to advertising to provide his revenue. He competes for advertising dollars with the other Canadian media such as daily and weekly newspapers, magazines and billboards. He also competes with U.S. border stations and with overflow advertising from the United States. If the economy is buoyant, and advertising expenditures increase each year, he can look forward to his share of the larger expenditures. A new and influential medium such as television has shown rapid annual increase in revenue as the number of TV sets and TV stations increased, and as advertisers discovered the ability of television to sell goods. Within a few years the skyrocketing curve of TV advertising revenue can be expected to level out.

It must be recognized that the conditions under which a broadcasting license is issued set limits and restrictions on the freedom of the broadcaster to secure revenue.

For example, certain types of financial advertising are not permitted. Beer and wine companies can sponsor programs, but with the advertising message limited to the name of the company and the product. There is no analogous regulation for beer and wine advertising in the United

States. Liquor may not be advertised at all in Canada; this is also true for the United States.

All drug product advertising is carefully checked by the BBG and the Department of National Health and Welfare.

The length of the television commercial announcement for non-Canadian, sponsored programs is regulated according to the following scale:

Length of Program (Minutes)	Length of Advertising Message (Minutes and Seconds)
5	1:15
10	2:10
15	3:00
20	3:30
25	4:00
30	4:15
40	5:00
45	5:45
60	7:00

Slightly higher commercial limits are allowed for sponsored Canadian television shows.

Radio stations are allowed 250 minutes (4 hours, 10 minutes) for commercial messages between 6:00 a.m. and midnight (18 hours). The total amount of commercial time during one week must not exceed 1500 minutes.

Radio stations are now required to file annually with the BBG "a statement covering the previous fiscal year and showing how each station has promoted and ensured the greater use of Canadian talent".

The effort to assure Canadian content and character in television is largely the story of the "55 per cent Canadian content" regulation established by the BBG.

The BBG began with a 45 per cent Canadian content provision for television stations and networks. It set a date by which this minimum was to be raised to 55 per cent. There were delays and postponements in enforcing the 55 per cent minimum, as a result of complaints from private stations that it was economically impossible to achieve this figure. The definition of Canadian content is also so curious, so flexible, that it is possible to meet the letter of the requirement with very much less than 55 per cent of actual Canadian programming. Credit is given to Commonwealth programs, to programs from France, to certain "important" world events regardless of who originates the program.

The 55 per cent Canadian content regulation refers to the time factor alone; it says nothing about the quality of Canadian programming. It simply provides an illustration of how difficult, how impossible, it is to secure high standards of broadcasting through laws and regulations alone.

In May of 1962, when the CBC repeated its annual sweep of the Ohio State Broadcasting Awards with 21 awards, private radio station CKVL, Verdun, in the first submissions by a French-language station, won two awards. With certain exceptions, the private radio and television stations have not been noted for distinguished broadcasting, for support of Canadian talent, or for the introduction of innovations in broadcasting. *The Fowler Report* said: "With notable exceptions, the private stations have done relatively little to encourage Canadian talent. . . . many could do more than they have done and yet be leagues away from anything resembling bankruptcy."

Yet, there was no doubt in the mind of the Royal Commissioners that there was a permanent place for the private broadcaster on the Canadian scene:

It is unlikely that an entirely publicly owned broadcasting system could give as good local and community service throughout Canada as is now provided by having a number of independent local units in the system. This is one of the principal reasons why we are strongly of the opinion that the continued presence of private elements in the system should be recognized and placed beyond uncertainty and doubt.

In affirming the continuing role of the private stations, *The Fowler Report* also asked for higher standards of performance:

We think that the presence of private elements in our broadcasting system should be accepted as valuable and permanent; but that the performance level of private stations should be a high one to justify the grant to them of valuable public rights—higher in fact than it has been, with some notable exceptions, in the past.

The problem of encouraging private broadcasters to higher standards of performance has so far defied solution. As Dr. Dawson says: "Regulations can, and do, dampen the effects of extremes to which incentives tend to drive private broadcasters, but regulations can have only limited effects when they are working against market forces."

A much sharper critic, Chester Wilmot, in an article in *Canadian Art,* writes: ". . . not *Critically Speaking,* nor anything else for that matter, has been able to do anything about private broadcasting in this country—except, perhaps, to ignore it."

As late as 1957, the private broadcasters continued to express their fear that Canada might revert to the recommendation of *The Aird Report* of 1929 that all broadcasting in Canada be nationalized.

With *The Fowler Report* and the Broadcasting Act of 1958, it has now been made perfectly clear that the Canadian system is to remain a mixed system, made up of public and private components.

What we are witnessing today is not a struggle for survival of the private broadcaster, but a battle over the roles to be played by the public and the private sectors of broadcasting.

The picture is complicated further by the fact that a considerable number of private radio and television stations are network affiliates of the CBC. This implies a close link between the public corporation and certain private stations. There is also, for the first time, a private network operating in the field of television, with nine affiliated stations. Existence of this network and of 165 private radio stations that are not affiliated with any network, makes it hard to continue with the thesis stated so frequently by *The Fowler Report* that we have "a single broadcasting system" of which all Canadian radio and television stations, public and private, form integral parts.

If it can no longer be claimed that the private broadcaster must live in fear of complete nationalization, it is possible that the shoe is now on the other foot. Having gained the separate regulatory body which they long sought, having been granted private television licenses for "second stations" in key communities, and having established a private television network, there are some private broadcasters who hope that a favourable political climate may make it possible to largely eliminate public broadcasting.

The first step which these private broadcasters propose is that the CBC retire completely from the field of commercial broadcasting. This, in their view, will leave the Corporation free to concentrate on its responsibility of providing a national service.

The next step is for the CBC to sell those stations which it owns to private broadcasters. This will relieve the government of a heavy investment, and again the responsibilities of the CBC will be reduced so that it can concentrate on creating Canadian programs.

The end result is a situation long advocated by Richard Lewis, editor and publisher of *Canadian Broadcaster,* a publication which has served for more than 20 years as the unofficial journal of the private broadcasters. Mr. Lewis suggests that the CBC should become a program producing agency, similar to the National Film Board. In order to obtain distribution of its programs, the CBC would have to rely on the BBG, which, by regulation would presumably require the private stations to carry certain CBC programs at certain times.

With such views being openly voiced and printed by those on the private side of broadcasting it is not surprising that the president of the CBC is now expressing in public the Corporation's desire to own and operate its own television stations at key points in every province.

The private broadcaster has a license that is good for a maximum of five years, providing he obeys the Broadcasting Act and the regulations of the BBG. In Britain, the BBC has traditionally operated on a 10-year charter. What is most lacking in the Canadian broadcasting scene is the element of stability. The CBC should have its role clarified, and it should have a five-year or preferably a 10-year charter and the assurance of statutory funds to carry out the task assigned to it. Lacking this, we are faced with a constant battle between the private and the public sector. Where once the private sector had a fear of being ousted through a program of complete nationalization, now it is the public sector that faces a campaign to gradually diminish the importance of the role which it plays.

The reference to the National Film Board is interesting. The NFB produces many award-winning documentary and animated films. They have won for Canada an enviable world reputation in this field. But because there is no provision for the regular showing of these films in the theatres of Canada, relatively few Canadians ever manage to see NFB products. Some films made by the NFB are shown on the CBC; they have reached far more Canadians in this way than they ever have through the theatres.

Canadian Association of Broadcasters

The Canadian Association of Broadcasters (which was known for a number of years as the Canadian Association of Radio and Television Broadcasters) is the association of private broadcasters in which most private stations have membership. The CAB maintains an office in Ottawa, with T. J. Allard as Executive Vice-President. President of the organization currently is Don Jamieson, a Newfoundland broadcaster.

The CAB represents the private broadcasters at Royal Commissions, Parliamentary Committees, and maintains contact with the BBG. It arranges for private broadcast representatives to sit on various joint committees set up by the BBG.

The CAB got along very badly with the Fowler Commission. Officials of the CAB have expressed criticism of this Commission, and of its findings. This is understandable when we read in *The Fowler Report* the comment that the CAB (then known as the CARTB) was basing its case on "devious propaganda wrapped in colourful verbiage".

The Fowler Report states:

". . . the CARTB has issued much one-sided or misleading information on the true nature and functioning of the present system of broadcasting in Canada, and this propaganda has largely gone unanswered by the CBC. The outcome has been to give shape in the public mind to analogies based on incomplete knowledge or insufficient reflection, to enroll the Canadian instinct for freedom behind hidden mercenary motives and to foment misunderstanding and confusion among the well-meaning."

In discussions with the writer, the view was expressed by a CAB official that the CBC and the private stations are not in fact equals before the BBG. The CBC is in a sense a senior partner. It has specific, serious responsibilities assigned to it by Parliament. This must be recognized by all. While the law provides that there shall be a CBC to perform certain essential functions, it provides that, after that, there may also be allowed private stations.

The representative of the CAB continued that he would like to see the CBC provided with sufficient funds on a

RADIO
National Network Service

Two radio networks serve Canadians; one English and one French.

Networks are made up of stations owned by the CBC, plus privately owned stations affiliated as part of the national service.

RADIO STATIONS

108 AM

LANGUAGE

78 ENGLISH | **30 FRENCH**

OWNERSHIP

CBC 28 PUBLIC | **80 PRIVATE**

NOT CONNECTED TO NATIONAL SERVICE

129 AM | **36 FM**

NOTES:

- The information in these charts comes from a "Fact Sheet" dated March 12, 1963, prepared by the CBC in consultation with the BBG and the Department of Transport.

- The CBC also owns and operates 98 low power relay transmitters. Also part of the nation's broadcasting service are 5 FM stations, 5 shortwave stations and 1 non-network AM station, all owned and operated by the CBC.

TELEVISION
National Network Service

An English and a French television network serve Canadians with the programs of the national service.

TV STATIONS

61

LANGUAGE

48 ENGLISH | **13** FR.

OWNERSHIP

CBC **14** PUBLIC | **47** PRIVATE

NOT CONNECTED TO NATIONAL SERVICE

12 ENGLISH | **1** FR.

NOTES:

- Of the 13 TV stations not connected with the national service, 9 form the CTV private English television network. In January, 1963, application was made for a private French television network.

- To distribute TV programs to areas remote from manned TV stations, the CBC operates 6 network relay stations and 10 rebroadcasting stations, the private affiliates operate 29 rebroadcasting stations, and the private supplementary stations operate 33 rebroadcasting stations.

statutory basis, so that it could make plans for a 10-year period, without being dependent on the whims of Parliament for an annual grant each year, and could provide coast-to-coast service with its own facilities. IIe would like the CBC freed in this way from the necessity to seek any commercial revenue.

In short, the CAB representative favoured for Canada two completely separate broadcasting systems; the one to be entirely public and non-commercial, the other to be entirely privately-owned and commercial. In this way, said the representative of CAB, it would be possible to offer the audience a true alternative set of programs. Under present conditions of competition, the CBC is often offering the same type of program at the same time as the competitive private station.

Can Canada afford two systems? Yes, said the CAB representative, if we are realistic. New and inexpensive production methods could be developed. Production could be concentrated in three main centres: Montreal, Toronto and Vancouver. Other stations could be merely retransmission centres.

The representative of the CAB was strongly opposed to a Royal Commission at the present time. It is a great drain on the time, energy and resources of key people in all broadcasting organizations. In his view, the industry needs a breathing spell so that it can get some work done. They would prefer to see a small study group of specialists established; possibly a five-man group with representatives from BBG, CBC, CAB, the Department of Transport and the Community Antenna Association.

The broadcasting industry has been too-much investigated. It is always on the defense against attack. The people involved in broadcasting cannot go about their work properly when they are constantly being called upon to justify their existence. These were some of the views expressed by a representative of the CAB.

The CAB, in addition to providing the lobbying and public relations services for its members, performs certain public service functions. Since 1944, the Radio Bureau of CAB has provided the facilities for "Report from Parliament Hill". This program permits members of Parliament to report to their constituents through their local private radio station by means of recorded broadcasts arranged by the CAB Radio Bureau. Unfortunately not all radio stations and not all members of Parliament make use of this excellent service.

Since 1961, the CAB has been the main sponsor of the Dominion Drama Festival, the annual country-wide competition for amateur theatrical groups. In addition to putting up a substantial sum of money to finance the event, members of the CAB contribute considerable broadcast time to Festival publicity. In particular, they bring to the attention of their audience the local drama group which is participating in the national competition.

The CAB deserves much credit for encouraging Canadian dramatic talent in this way. However, it is hard to take seriously the argument that this is a means of developing future talent for broadcasting. The record of the private broadcasters in the employment of Canadian talent of any kind is poor. According to the figures reported by the Dominion Bureau of Statistics for 1960, the private radio stations with net advertising revenue of $46 million spent $1.4 million in artist and other talent fees. Private television stations, with $23.4 million in net advertising revenue in 1960, spent less than half a million dollars for artist and other talent fees. There is little evidence to suggest that the situation is changing.

In a speech to the Canadian Association of Broadcasters in March, 1962, Don Jamieson, President of the Association spoke of the need for a new national broadcasting policy. He deplored the open antagonism which often exists be-

tween the private broadcasters and those who support the
CBC. For Canada, neither a completely non-commercial
public system of broadcasting, nor a completely private
commercial system of broadcasting, is possible or likely. The
present problem is to define the roles which each should
play.

Mr. Jamieson is prepared to admit that there is a place
for the CBC, but he wants the CBC's responsibilities re-
defined.

The introduction of many new elements requires that a new
look be taken at how the system is operating. Honesty and
objectivity compel the conviction that the CBC must re-
examine its "mandate". Obviously the Corporation ought
to, and will continue to play, a vital role in national development. Thoughtful, reasonable people will disabuse their
minds of any thoughts to the contrary. There is a need, however, to clarify the nature of the national broadcasting
service which the CBC has a special responsibility to provide. The relationship between public and private elements,
in broadcasting, must be re-defined and clearly understood.
For it cannot be forgotten that, in television in particular,
the CBC simply cannot function, as a truly national service, without the willing help, and co-operation of many
privately-owned stations.

Mr. Jamieson indicates that the private broadcasters,
possessed of much knowledge and experience in the field,
should be prepared to devote their talents to achieving the
best utilization of the total broadcasting facilities of the
nation. He says: "Both public, and private broadcasters, as
well as others who are part of this 'great debate', must seek
to find the answers. There is a job for each of us to do and
we must find the most efficient way of doing it, and of
producing the best results."

VI

CTV

CTV

On December 8, 1960, the BBG approved the application of S. W. Caldwell of Toronto, for authority to establish a private television network in Canada. Among the requirements were that the new network would have affiliation agreements with a minimum of six stations, and that these stations would clear a minimum of 10 hours of reserved time per week, for which the network would provide the programs.

On October 1, 1961, CTV Television Network Ltd. began operations with eight affiliates[1]. In August, 1962, a ninth station—CHAB-TV at Moose Jaw—joined CTV.
During the first year the network averaged about 10 hours of programs per week. Programs were distributed by videotape, while arrangements were made for linking the private network by micro-wave.

During the first year of operation, a high proportion of the Canadian programs produced by the CTV network were quiz programs, or what network officials prefer to call "game shows". The reason for this was partly economic, since this is a relatively inexpensive type of program to produce. For its second year of operation, 1962-63, CTV produced 24 hours a week of network programs, with a better balance of programming.

The officials of the CTV network estimate that they are capable of reaching some 70 per cent of the Canadian television audience with their present "Big City Network". From a commercial point of view, this is the cream of the Canadian audience, since it covers the most densely populated urban areas of Canada.

----

[1]Vancouver — CHAN-TV
Calgary — CFCN-TV
Edmonton — CFRN-TV
Winnipeg — CJAY-TV
Toronto — CFTO-TV
Ottawa — CJOH-TV
Montreal — CFCF-TV
Halifax — CJCH-TV

In looking to the future, officials of the CTV network plan to increase the number of members to 15 stations in major markets, with satellites to cover other areas. They estimate that this arrangement would give CTV access to from 80 to 90 per cent of the available Canadian television audience. That coverage is the present limit of their plans. They do not consider that it would be economically practical to attempt greater extension of the network.

Affiliates which are added to CTV can join only in the following circumstances, according to present arrangements:
1. New private stations.
2. Private station affiliates of the CBC which receive permission from the BBG to leave that network, presumably because CBC network coverage to the area is available from other transmitters.
3. Private stations which are CBC affiliates which become disengaged from that network because CBC acquires a television transmitter of its own in that locality.

Obviously, the competition for affiliates between the private CTV network and the public CBC network could become a serious battle.

The officials of CTV[1] look forward, over a period of perhaps 10 years, to a two-stage development in the field of television:

Stage 1:   The CBC to be removed entirely from the field of commercial activity, on a gradual basis.

---

[1]The following are the directors of CTV Television Network Ltd.:
S. W. Caldwell, President
G. F. Keeble, Executive Vice-President
Sydney Hermant, President, Imperial Optical Company
D. M. Pringle, of Lash, Lash and Pringle
W. F. McLean, President, Canada Packers, Ltd.
F. S. Chalmers, President, MacLean-Hunter Publishing Company
K. B. Andras, of Andras, Hatch & McCarthy
John Bassett, Chairman of Board, CFTO-TV
L. E. Moffat, Vice-President of Channel Television Ltd.
R. K. Martin, President of Martin, Lucas & Company
E. F. MacDonald, President of CJCH Ltd., Halifax

Stage 2: Stations owned by the CBC to be sold to private owners. When this stage is reached, the CBC will remain as a producer of Canadian programs; these programs will be carried by private stations on instructions from the BBG.

Officials of CTV were among the only private broadcasters to challenge the idea of a fixed percentage of "Canadian Content". They still question whether the ruling achieves the objective which it seeks. The quantitative requirement makes no provision for quality or variety in Canadian content. It could serve to encourage the production of low-cost, poor quality programs which would have little to recommend them but the fact that they met the Canadian content requirements.

A satisfactory alternative to the present Canadian Content requirements has not yet been arrived at. It has been suggested that one alternative might be to require a station or a network to devote a certain proportion of its total revenues, perhaps 10 per cent, to Canadian talent. This might result in the production of some outstanding programs. However, a broadcaster could pour all his dollars into one or two outstanding Canadian productions per year, and while the quality might be exceptional, the time involved might be a very small fraction of the program schedule while the remaining time could be devoted to imported programs, entirely non-Canadian in content.

In Britain, the Pilkington Commission criticized the BBC for the manner in which they competed with the private producers of the ITV. There was a tendency to compete for audience by offering the same type of programs at the same hours. This deprived the audience of the opportunity for real choice, which is one of the advantages to be gained from having more than one program source. This same criticism may be applied in Canada. Urged on by the recommendation of the Fowler Commission that they compete more effectively, and by a desire to achieve good audience ratings in competition with the private TV stations and network, the CBC has too often presented popular American syndicated programs, to compete with similar programs on private television.

The CTV network must observe the Canadian Content regulations in preparing its program plans. However, in a number of ways the CTV network is quite different from the CBC network and from the three major networks in the United States.

The nine affiliates of CTV own shares in the network. More important, they have a considerable voice in deciding the number and time periods of the programs for which they will allot network time on their stations.

Unlike most networks, CTV owns no stations and has no studios or production facilities of its own. It operates a program control centre at its Toronto headquarters, and it makes use, in certain instances, of the studio and production facilities of member stations. But, for the most part, CTV rents the studio facilities it requires and hires outside producers or production companies to prepare those CTV network programs which are not purchased in film cans from outside Canada. However, a major financial commitment of CTV is a $12 million contract for the micro-wave facilities which link the stations of the network.

CTV has undertaken to broadcast 24 hours per week of network programs during the 1962-1963 season. There is no place in its plans for unsponsored programs. All programs fed to its affiliate stations are available for commercial sponsorship. Since it is often in unsponsored programs that a station or a network can test new program ideas, writers, producers and talent, CTV is handicapped in the lack of these opportunities to experiment. Some program ideas are created by member stations and then adopted by CTV and put on the network. Considerable use is made of the facilities and personnel of member stations in preparing network programs. At January 1, 1963, the entire staff of CTV, including executives, salesmen, producers and secretaries, consisted of 57 persons.

The economics of CTV's present operations do not allow for unsponsored programs. In time, as the network expands, as it increases the number of hours of network broadcasting, it is possible that its revenues will be sufficient to allow it to employ a larger production staff for planning and producing unsponsored experimental programs, as well as tested programs which can be assured of a substantial audience, and are therefore of greater interest to the advertiser.

At its present stage of development, the private television network—CTV—is an essentially commercial operation. Perhaps, in the distant future, there will be time for concern with such questions as a balanced schedule of programs, public service activities, serving the interests of various minority groups, educational television. But, at present, the concern is with maximizing coverage, improving the program ratings, and pushing sales to the point where CTV will begin to show a profit to those individuals who have invested their capital in the enterprise, and the member private stations, also part owners.

VII

THE UNDEFENDED BORDER

THE UNDEFENDED BORDER

In the late 1920's and early 1930's it was the flood of broadcasts from the United States pouring into Canada that provided the stimulus for a national service that would supply Canadian programming for Canadians.

The threat of flooding is always with us. Every dike that is built quickly springs dozens of leaks. Here are just some of the important ways in which the competition of United States broadcasting appears:

1. United States border stations which concentrate their attention on the Canadian audience.

    Station KVOS-TV, Bellingham, Washington, directs its attention to the Vancouver area.

2. Broadcasts packaged in the United States on record, transcription, film and videotape which are sold in Canada for use on Canadian networks and stations.

    The "Screen Gems" organization offers scores of programs such as "Father Knows Best", "Route 66", "Naked City", "The Flintstones", some in French as well as in English.

3. Canadian stations which are affiliated with United States networks and carry considerable segments of the United States program schedule.

    Radio Station CJAD, Montreal, which is affiliated with the Columbia Broadcasting System is in this category.

4. United States network programs which are carried live on Canadian networks.

    The Sunday evening "Ed Sullivan Show" which is carried by the CBC network has a large Canadian audience.

5. TV production crews which come into Canada at the invitation of Canadian stations or production companies

79

to produce "Canadian" programs, the ideas and production skills for which are provided from across the border. The "Pierre Berton Hour" which is produced by the "Screen Gems" organization falls into this category, and many "game" shows which are carbon copies of United States originals.

6. Minority United States ownership of Canadian broadcasting stations.

There is substantial United States minority interest in CFTO-TV, Toronto, for example.

7. United States ownership, total, majority or minority of TV film sales companies, sales agencies which represent Canadian and United States broadcasting stations, trade papers and other institutions serving the broadcasting industry.

The A. C. Nielsen Company, which provides radio and television audience reports through its Canadian division may be cited in this connection.

In broadcasting, as in other phases of life in Canada, serious problems are created by United States competition. With a vast domestic audience, the broadcasters of the United States turn out an abundance of programs with mass appeal. These programs are sold for use in Canada at prices that are a fraction of what it would cost to produce equivalent programs in Canada, with Canadian talent. This represents a form of "dumping", since the cost of the program has been amortized by revenues from United States stations.

Let us examine a few examples of United States penetration and influence in some detail. Station KVOS is a U.S. station, an affiliate of the CBS network, licensed to transmit from Bellingham, in the state of Washington. Bellingham is a small community of some 30,000 homes that could hardly support its own TV station. But Bellingham is only 40 air miles from Vancouver, B.C. In fact, KVOS directs its main attention to the Vancouver market and is frequently the Number 1 station in Vancouver.

On a Wednesday night in November, 1962, according to the report of McDonald Research Limited, this is what Vancouverites were tuned to at 10:30 p.m.

Station	Program	Number of Homes
KVOS (U.S.)	Detectives	58,000
CHAN (private)	News, Sports	31,000
CBUT (CBC)	Formative Years (Dramatized documentary series about Canada's history prior to Confederation)	23,000

KVOS claims only 350,000 population within its signal area on the U.S. side of the border; it claims more than 1,000,000 people within range of its signal on the Canadian side of the border.

KVOS has a company registered in Canada, KVOS-TV (B.C.) Ltd., with offices in Vancouver. It sells to Canadian merchants and accepts Canadian funds in payment for its services. It maintains in Vancouver a sales staff, a merchandising staff and complete staff and facilities for the production of TV commercials.

This is probably the most extreme example of an over-the-border operation. However, it has a Canadian counterpart at Windsor, Ontario where the Canadian station, CKLW-TV, directs much of its attention to the much more populous city of Detroit, Michigan, which is right on its doorstep.

The problem of the U.S. border station reappears at other points along the border; at Winnipeg, in the Niagara, Hamilton, Lake Ontario and Toronto areas, and to some extent in the Montreal area.

Basically, television waves follow the line of sight so that the height of the transmitting tower, geography and topography are among the important factors in determining the coverage of any TV station. The flat lands of the prairies and the waters of the Great Lakes present unobstructed routes for TV signals from south of the border.

It is a minor problem in Montreal, partly for language reasons, and partly because the border stations in this area are small operations.

According to the reports of McDonald Research Limited, this was what Montrealers were watching on a Friday evening in November, 1962 at 10:30 p.m.

Station	Program	Number of Homes
CFTM (French-Private)	Echoes Vedettes (Behind the scenes in the French Canadian world of entertainment in Montreal)	147,000
CBMT (English-CBC)	Candid Camera (A U.S. program giving reactions of the "Man in the street" to unusual and amusing situations)	80,000
CFCF (English-Private)	News, Sports	65,000
CBFT (French-CBC)	Premier Plan (Studies in depth of political situations and social problems)	64,000
WCAX (U.S.)	Eyewitness	10,000

In the Toronto area, the Buffalo, N.Y., stations with their major network affiliations, offer much more serious competition. According to the same source, this was the TV viewing situation in Toronto at 10:30 on a Friday evening in November, 1962:

Station	Program	Number of Homes
WGR (U.S.)	Jack Paar (Interviews)	109,000
CBLT (CBC)	Candid Camera (a U.S. program)	93,000
WKBW (U.S.)	Third Man (Dramatic program)	70,000
CFTO (Can.-Private)	News	41,000
WBEN (U.S.)	Eyewitness	32,000

Considerably more than half of the homes in Toronto were tuned to U.S. stations at this hour.

These are simply examples. The viewing situation changes from hour to hour, and survey results are approximations of the actual situation. However, these can be considered as realistic illustrations of the nature of the problem of the competition of U.S. border stations.

The ease with which the waves of broadcasting stations cross the international border has also resulted in an audience for the programs of the CBC in the United States. Some of the most appreciative audience mail received by the CBC is from United States citizens who listen to its broadcasts from border stations. On occasion, letters are received from as far away as Virginia, Florida and Texas. In terms of numbers, these over-the-border listeners to the CBC probably represent a small, but discriminating, minority.

The problem is a sticky one. Canadians believe in freedom of communication. They also believe in the merits of competition. If U.S. stations have the power—electrical and otherwise—to divert the Canadian audience, then it is up to Canadian broadcasters and public authorities to face the challenge squarely. Better Canadian programs are one answer. But the high audience rating of some lower quality programs implies that there are other complex factors involved and that success in winning an audience is not inextricably bound up with quality of programming.

The competition of the U.S. border stations would represent a different type of problem if the programs they present were of high quality. But the chairman of the F.C.C., Newton N. Minow, has made frequent appeals for an improvement in what he termed the "vaste wasteland" of American television. Speaking in April, 1963 to the National Association of Broadcasters in Chicago, Mr. Minow referred to the flood of commercialism and the failure of the efforts at self-regulation. According to Mr. Minow, "A TV commercial is broadcast somewhere in the U.S. every 1.7 seconds. To figure out how often a radio commercial occurs would give a computer a nervous breakdown". Referring to the code established by the National Association of Broadcasters, Mr. Minow pointed out that only 38 per cent of radio stations and 70 per cent of TV stations subscribe to the code. Even stations that subscribe to the N.A.B. code, do not observe this effort at industry self-regulation. Said Minow: "Though you have established reasonable standards for yourselves you have demonstrated neither the capacity nor the will to enforce them. You can no longer have it both ways. You cannot subscribe in principle and ignore it in practice. Self-regulation cannot become self-deception". Mr. Minow said to the broadcasters, "We will continue to prod your consciences, to goad your ideals, to disturb your sleep". As head of the F.C.C. Mr. Minow can deliver stern lectures, but as matters now stand he lacks the authority to do more than this. His resignation as Chairman of the FCC took effect as of June 11, 1963.

As we know, broadcasting is a powerful influence on our thinking and on our lives. Obviously, Canadians should be able to enjoy the best of the broadcasting produced by the United States, Britain and every other nation that has something outstanding to offer. However, unless basic elements of broadcasting are Canadian, the sights and sounds that bring us our picture of the world around us will reflect a foreign, rather than a Canadian, point of view.

VIII

THE PEOPLE, THE PRESS
AND PARLIAMENT

THE PEOPLE, THE PRESS AND PARLIAMENT

After we have talked about the BBG, the CBC, the private stations, the CTV network, French-language broadcasting . . . finally we get around to talking about the most important group of all, the audience.

A fine distinction could be drawn between the Canadian public at large and the audience for broadcasting in Canada. But, in these times almost every house in the land has at least one radio set, and nine out of ten have a television set. Whether the individual Canadian owns or does not own broadcast receiving equipment, whether he listens to the broadcasts of the CBC and the private stations or not, he still has an important stake in broadcasting.

Offsetting to some extent the competition of television, radio has extended its audience through car radios and via transistor sets which go with some people wherever they go. Multiple radio set ownership is a common phenomenon in many homes, with the average number of radio sets per family now standing at slightly more than two.

In January 1963, the number of homes in Canada with television was 4,120,000; the number of homes with radio was 4,470,000. The members of the audience have invested far more dollars in receiving sets than the entire broadcasting industry, public and private, has invested in studios and broadcasting equipment. The amount that the members of the audience spend to operate their radio and television receivers has been estimated at *$400 million per year;* this covers depreciation, maintenance, electricity and insurance. Again, the money spent by the audience is considerably more than the amount spent by advertisers and by the government on all the programs, studios, transmitters, staff and transmission lines for *all* Canadian radio and television!

In the United States, with minor exceptions, all broadcasting is supported by advertising. Yet, it would pay us to look around the world, and examine the situation in other countries. The example and influence of the U.S. broadcaster has extended into the Caribbean, and into Latin America. But, in Europe, Asia and Africa most countries operate on the basis of a license fee levied on each radio and television set, which provides funds for the broadcasting service. In most countries of the world, advertising by radio and television is either prohibited, or is closely controlled.

For example, France continues to bar all advertising. In Italy and West Germany limited periods are allowed for commercial announcements, but these are segregated completely from the regular program schedule. Britain began and continued for many years with all broadcasting in the hands of the publicly-owned British Broadcasting Corporation. More recently, Britain experimented with a second TV network and with commercially sponsored television broadcasts.

It is worthy of note that all commercial television in Britain is handled through a government agency, the Independent Television Authority, which owns and operates the transmitting stations. The programs are provided by commercial program companies under contract to the Authority.

As a result of the investigation of the Pilkington Royal Commission, the British government issued a White Paper recommending that the Independent Television Authority should take on a more positive role; it recommended that the I.T.A. should control network programming, should supervise the buying and selling of programs, and should assume responsibility for the "shape, content, balance and quality of the service as a whole". Says the White Paper:

The Government is concerned to prevent the danger not only of excessive violence but also excessive triviality in the treatment of programmes. In the last resort these are matters which must depend on the vigilance of the broadcasting authorities. Prescription by legislation of the detailed programme standards would be ineffective.

In Britain, as in most countries, a license fee on radio and television sets is in force. Under this situation, which formerly applied in Canada, the beneficiaries of broadcasting contribute directly to finance the service. In Canada, the license fee is considered a nuisance, and a source of trouble for the political parties. It is considered much easier to take the money required to support broadcasting from the general tax fund than to ask the members of the audience directly for an annual fee to support the service. This would be a good point at which to recall the words of a 19th century French economist, Frédéric Bastiat, who wrote: "Everyone wants to live at the expense of the state. They forget that the state lives at the expense of everyone."

In broadcasting, one critical criterion of program value is audience response. The members of the audience look and listen, they enjoy and benefit from what they see and hear, or they do not.

So, the really important decisions in broadcasting concern the type and quality of programs, the range, the variety, the balance between the various elements in the schedule of a station, or of a network.

A very influential factor in the life of the private broadcaster is the program rating. This is a statistical report that indicates the size of the audience for particular programs, on particular stations, at particular times. The ratings are based on surveys of samples of the potential audience. A number of different program rating services are available in Canada.

The program rating services are made use of by advertisers in determining the "cost per thousand" for reaching members of the audience. Two extreme positions may be stated: (1) a high rating tells us nothing about the value or impact of a particular program; it does tell us that a substantial audience was available for the particular program; (2) a program may be considered of high quality, but if it has an extremely low rating, this indicates that the audience consisted of only a few people, and the total influence of the program is therefore low. Ratings should not be the sole consideration, nor should they be ignored. They are a quantitive measurement of the size of the audience, by no means exact, but worth some attention if the sampling is conscientiously carried out, the data competently analyzed and the results honestly reported.

Even in Canada, television audiences can run into the millions. It is therefore possible that a program with a low rating may still reach 100,000 or 200,000 people. When we consider the cost of providing a concert or a lecture of quality to this number of people, it becomes apparent that even a program with a low audience rating may bring material of quality to people in all parts of Canada more speedily and more economically than any other available method.

The CBC has a well-staffed audience research division. Its members analyze program ratings, but not just to determine how much it cost to "buy" listeners, per thousand. They combine the study of program ratings with many other types of research in an effort to plan better programs and better schedules for the several networks operated by the CBC.

There is not one audience for radio and television, but many audiences. These audiences vary in composition from area to area. The range of broadcasting outlets available also differ greatly; in a large centre like Toronto, the audience may have a dozen strong radio signals to choose from and as many as eight television channels. A number of these will be signals from neighbouring points in the United States. In other locations, the audience in a geographical pocket may be forced to select its programs from one radio and one television station. The approximately three per cent of Canadians who are not within range of

Canadian radio, or the approximately six per cent who are not within the range of Canadian television fall outside this discussion entirely.

Where there are many radio and television channels in operation, the audience *may* exercise a wider discretion. But, if all or most of the stations offer exactly the same type of program fare at the same time, the extent of choice may be more apparent than real. In the remote areas, the audience is highly dependent on the local broadcasting facilities for a service that will meet the full range of its needs and interests.

The Canadian Broadcasting League

A tally of the groups that made written or verbal presentations to the Aird, Massey and Fowler Commissions, gives a clue to the number and diversity of Canadian organization with an apparent interest in broadcasting. Included in the list are many consumer, farm, labour, educational, religious and women's groups.

Among the many groups interested in broadcasting appears the Canadian Radio League, founded in the late 1920's by Graham Spry and the late Alan Plaunt. The Radio League was active while the Aird Commission sat in 1929, was revived for a time during the mid-1950's as the Canadian Radio and Television League, and was reorganized again in 1960 as the Canadian Broadcasting League. The League has been at times extremely active and influential, at other times dormant. It has always stressed the cardinal importance of a national broadcasting service for Canadians. It remains firm in this conviction. Members of the League are sometimes accused of being long-haired, egg-headed intellectuals. They have also been accused of being uncritical lobbyists for the CBC.

One weakness of the League is that it is top-heavy. Leaders of many national organizations have taken an active interest in the League, and have taken positions on the subject of broadcasting; in many cases their membership knows or cares little about the subject, and has not been informed or consulted.

Canada is fortunate in having a Broadcasting League, in spite of alleged shortcomings, and despite the barbs thrown by critics of the League. While the audience is the most important element in broadcasting, in no other country of the world, to the writer's knowledge, is there a strong, effective association representing the citizens, the listeners, and the viewers.

Possibly the most important functions the Canadian Broadcasting League can perform are:

— education of the general public (beginning with the hundreds of thousands of Canadians who belong to member organizations) to the realities and possibilities of broadcasting in Canada.

— encouragement of member organizations to study broadcasting, to consult their membership on the subject, and to make representations to the appropriate body: to the member of Parliament, the BBG, the CBC, the private station.

— lastly, the League can itself undertake studies, issue informational material, and in consultation with the member organizations, make direct representations to the governmental authorities that regulate, control or operate broadcasting.

The Press

Nowhere in Canada is there to be found a medium of expression to which one can look for objective analysis and comment on broadcasting, unless it is in some of the learned journals of the universities.

We are fortunate in having a strong, lively daily press in Canada. But, whether or not there is direct influence on the editor, reporter and commentator, we cannot ignore the fact the newspapers are keen competitors with the broadcast medium for advertising dollars. To complicate matters further many newspapers and magazines in Canada own, or are financially interested in radio and television stations.

For these reasons, while there is often comment and opinion expressed by the press on the subject of broadcasting, one can question whether the points of view expressed are sufficiently unbiased and disinterested for the best critical purposes.

As a rival of broadcasting, the newspaper or magazine may welcome and encourage an atmosphere of crisis and impending doom in broadcasting. As the owner of private broadcasting interests, a newspaper or magazine may challenge the operations of the CBC as a waste of the taxpayers' money, and may urge that the CBC get out of the commercial broadcasting field and stick to the more dignified task of providing shows that will inform, inspire and unite Canadians.

Despite these strictures, there are some editors, commentators and critics who do write fairly objective comments about broadcasting in the popular press. But, on the whole, editorial and news treatment of broadcasting in the papers must be taken with a large grain of salt.

Recently, there has been established a Canadian Institute of Communications with an office in Ottawa. The organization, under the directorship of Rev. J. W. Mole, of the University of Ottawa, has recruited members in many branches of the mass media industries. A quarterly journal, *Canadian Communications,* contains articles in both French and English and is now in the second year. The organization is still in its early stages, and is intended as a coordinating body that will encourage research projects, but will not undertake such projects on its own.

There is lacking in Canada a communications research institute, in a university setting. Communications is now a subject that occupies the attention of more than a hundred American universities; there are a score or more of special institutes for teaching and research in communications. So far they are but monuments to the divorce between the finest scholarly publications and utterances and the lax practice of too many U.S. broadcasters. It is to be hoped that a Canadian institute would provide ". . . hard factual information to displace the hearsay speculation and downright nonsense that at present passes for knowledge about some of the more important broadcasting problems in Canada today".

In the near future, Parliament is going to be asked to render some new decisions on the subject of broadcasting. In the House of Commons there are few men who have taken a special interest in the subject. Mr. George C. Nowlan, who has reported to Parliament on the activities of BBG and CBC, is one of the better informed persons. Mr. G. E. Halpenny who, as Secretary of State, reported to Parliament on the BBG and the CBC and who served as Chairman of the 1959 Parliamentary Committee on Broadcasting recently resigned from his cabinet post. In the Liberal ranks, L. B. Pearson and J. W. Pickersgill have taken an active part in debates on broadcasting. For the New Democratic Party, Douglas Fisher has been an active participant in debates on this topic.

There are, in fact, few people in Parliament who have any special knowledge or insight into the problems of broadcasting. There are members who are considered specialists on agriculture, economics, trade, defense and other topics of vital importance to the nation. Broadcasting ranks in importance with any of these topics, but there is not a single member of Parliament who can be considered an expert on broadcasting.

Broadcasting, as we have seen, has been much investigated. With the years, broadcasting has become bigger, more expensive, much more complex. Problems are technological, involving engineering and electronics, economics, law, politics, psychology. The range and complexity is greater than even this list of tags would indicate. Broadcasting is information, education, entertainment, and also a means of advertising. The range of talents and skills involved in the world of entertainment is vast, and few of these submit to the type of quantitative controls familiar to the business man or the civil servant. "Show business" is something very special. Broadcasting of news and special events, the discussion of public affairs, these involve a new branch of journalism. Radio brought "spoken journalism", now television involves a journalism that combines vision, voice, movement and actuality. The graphic treatment of the news that once took days to reach the newsreel audience in the theatre, now reaches the television audience in hours, minutes, or even seconds.

Education is a formidable word. We are only beginning to learn that there is no barrier that separates entertainment from education. The two can be highly compatible. With radio and television it is possible to reach audiences greater than all the classrooms of the nation combined. Material presented in an interesting way can be learned more readily. A great new challenge has been presented to the educator.

Some people talk about "sugar-coating the pill", of catching people off guard by slipping an informational or educational program between programs of entertainment. This view misses the mark. It also underestimates the audience. Properly presented, material of value to the individual can be entertaining as well as informative. The individual can derive much greater satisfaction from a program that leaves

him with something of value, than from repetitious material
with no real sustenance in it.

There is much talk about educational television, but
little activity and even less really adventuresome exper-
imentation. Education should be a part of the daily television schedule, not a ghetto or an annex of television. The
view expressed in the British White Paper of July, 1962,
which commented on the findings of the Pilkington Report
was:

While the Government fully agrees that television can do a
great deal more for education, it considers, as do the Committee, that such programs will best be provided as part of
the general programs and that it would be a mistake to hive
them off, at this stage at least, into an entirely separate
program insulated from the attractions of television in
general.

Broadcasting is the subject of much discussion and
controversy in Canada. It has been a contentious subject for
the past 30 years and more. It will probably continue to be
a lively topic of debate for many years, for the simple
reason that broadcasting continues to be a new, dynamic,
changing medium of communication, and one that influences our lives in a powerful fashion. We are still far
from being sure about how, or how much broadcasting
influences the lives of children and adults in Canada. But
while we have not yet measured the exact nature or extent
of the influence, we are certain that the influence on our
lives is enormous.

We are only beginning to understand, after five centuries,
the influence of Gutenberg and the invention of the print-
ing press. It is only three or four decades since the work of
Marconi began to blossom into a major form of human
communication; small wonder that we have not yet been
able to measure the full impact of the electronic revolution

on our society. No sooner had a print-oriented society begun to measure human attainment and potential in terms of ability to read and write, than along came a revolution in communication by whose means much can be learned—by ear and eye, through radio and television—by people with little or no literacy.

IX

LOOKING BACKWARD

LOOKING BACKWARD

A full-scale history of Canadian broadcasting has yet to be written. All that will be attempted here is to review briefly some of the main stages in the development of Canadian broadcasting.

Pioneer Days

On December 12, 1901, Guglielmo Marconi sat at a radio receiving set in St. John's, Newfoundland. Faintly but certainly he heard the first radio signal to cross the Atlantic, transmitted from the Marconi station at Poldhu in Cornwall, England.

At the time, radio was still a matter of Morse code pip signals. By 1918, broadcasting of the human voice had been achieved and the Marconi company was transmitting occasional programs over station XWA, Montreal, the first radio station in Canada. On November 4, 1920, this station received official authority to broadcast regular programs, and is today known to Montreal area listeners as CFCF.

The original licensing authority was the Minister of Defence. In 1923, the Department of Marine and Fisheries took over responsibility for broadcasting, and began issuing licenses to broadcasting stations. It also began to collect a $1 license fee from the owner of each receiving set.

The Unregulated Period

Most of the early radio stations were owned and backed by newspapers, or by stores interested in encouraging the sale of receiving sets. For the newspapers there was a two-fold interest: radio was a new and exciting topic of conversation, also radio was a potential competitor. A few far-sighted newspaper owners hedged against future events. They moved into this new field of communication, rather than allow it to fall into the hands of rivals.

The early stations were few in number, low in power and broadcast only intermittently. Two characteristically Canadian problems emerged from the start. First, there was the border problem. Some U.S. radio stations interfered with the signals of Canadian radio stations. Others attracted the attention of Canadian listeners away from Canadian stations. Concentration of population was another problem. Of the few Canadian stations in operation by 1931, more than half, by number and power, were crowded into Montreal and Toronto. Even these offered more U.S. than Canadian material. Four stations in Toronto and Montreal had wire connections with U.S. networks, which supplied about half their daily schedules. The rest of the schedules consisted mainly of imported recorded music, with the addition of news and the occasional live program. Canadians living in smaller communities and rural areas remote from the main centres of population were beyond the reach of the magic waves.

From several directions, pressures began to be exerted to do something about the regulation of radio broadcasting. In Britain, after several committees of parliament had investigated the question, the British Broadcasting Corporation was established and given a ten-year charter dating from January 1, 1927. In Canada, after the early period during which the main purpose of the broadcaster was to encourage people to buy receiving sets, the advertiser began to discover radio, and to both use and abuse this potent messenger. Interference from U.S. stations and the growth of networks in the U.S. which were reaching into Canada, these were matters of concern. Also, at least a few Canadians were concerned about the danger that radio could become a powerful and dangerous political tool in the hands of the party in power. There was a need to resolve the problem of how to take full advantage of the potential of broadcasting in a democracy, and at the same time prevent the abuse of the medium by unscrupulous politicians.

The Radio Department of the C.N.R.

Sir Henry Thornton, placed in charge of the rambling and debt-ridden, government-owned Canadian National Railways was looking for some means to publicize railway travel and encourage more passengers to use the C.N.R. He turned to radio, man's newest scientific break-through in communications, in his effort to bring railway travel into the news, and out of the red.

Thornton had the advantage of his own telegraph lines, which could also be used to transmit radio signals. A Radio Department of the C.N.R. was established. In 1923, on Christmas Day, the C.N.R. linked stations in Montreal and Ottawa, providing Canada with its first network broadcast.

The railway equipped Radio Cars with a uniformed attendant to tune the complicated, primitive equipment so that passengers could enjoy music and news as they journeyed. By 1930, when depression wiped out all such frills, the C.N.R. had 80 fully-equipped Radio Cars.

It was also necessary to provide programs, for there were few stations broadcasting on a regular schedule. The C.N.R. established some of its own stations, and in conjunction with other stations it extended its two-station network of 1923 to an eastern Canadian network in 1927, and by 1929 could boast facilities for Canadian broadcasts from one coast of the continent to the other. In 1929, the Toronto Symphony Orchestra was engaged to provide an "All Canada Symphony Hour" each Sunday afternoon.

This was part of a policy of presenting Canadian programs, for Canadian listeners. In 1930, dramatist Merrill Denison was commissioned to write a series of Canadian historical plays. A talented young man by the name of Tyrone Guthrie was brought from England to direct the series.

The Radio Department of the C.N.R. was a direct fore-runner of the Canadian Radio Broadcasting Commission, established in 1932, which evolved into the Canadian Broadcasting Corporation in 1936.

The foundations for the distinctively "Canadian way" of broadcasting were laid down by the Royal Commission appointed in 1928. Its report, named for its chairman, banker Sir John Aird, is known familiarly as the Aird Report; it appeared in a fateful year, 1929.

The Aird Report, like the report of many a Royal Commission, recommended many things which did not come about. The report recommended a highly autonomous broadcasting organization, along the lines of the BBC. It recommended that this national broadcasting system should acquire and operate all private stations. To finance this, it recommended both increased license fees from listeners, and a grant of funds from the government.

Two major events stood in the way of the accomplishment of these recommendations. One was the depression. The second was the Canadian constitution.

Because of the economic distress of the early 1930's, it was not considered an opportune time to buy out private stations with government funds, provide grants to a national broadcasting organization, and ask the economically distressed citizens for a higher license fee.

The provinces challenged the national government's rights to control broadcasting. In 1931, the Supreme Court of Canada decided in favour of the national government. The provinces disputed the matter further, and it was finally decided in favour of the national government by a verdict of the Judicial Committee of the Privy Council in 1932.

By the time the Parliamentary Committee of 1932 sat down to deal with the matter, delay and economic conditions resulted in a considerable watering-down of *The Aird Report* recommendations.

The Canadian Radio Broadcasting Commission (CRBC)

The desire for a national broadcasting service was still strong, however. In November, 1932, as a result of the work of the Parliamentary Committee, and of Parliament, there was established the Canadian Radio Broadcasting Commission. The head Commissioner was a well known Canadian literary figure, Hector Charlesworth. The three-man Commission took over the stations and staff of the C.N.R.'s radio department and set to work to establish a national radio broadcasting system. At the time, it was estimated that there were 600,000 receiving sets in Canada, and that about 40 per cent of the population was within range of the existing Canadian radio stations.

The Commission could build and purchase only a few stations with the small budget available to it from license fees on receiving sets, and from advertising revenue. It had no alternative but to rely heavily on private stations as affiliates, in order to spread its network to all parts of Canada. The cost of the wires to link the stations across Canada cut deeply into the budget.

In the four years of its life, the Commission accomplished a great deal. Particularly when we consider that the Commissioners were only part-time, and that they had very limited funds. But, beginning with 2 hours a week of broadcasting early in 1933, the CRBC was broadcasting on a regular schedule of 48 hours each week by the end of the year. For the guidance of the private stations, the Commission provided rules governing programs and advertising. Limits were set on the amount and type of advertising permitted, and arrangements were made with the Department of National Health to pass on all advertising for medical products. A Northern Messenger Service was begun for Canadians in the far north. In 1935, shortwave links with Britain and the Continent were established. By 1936, Canadian programs were available to half the Canadian popula-

tion, from Canadian stations. The national network consisted of 54 stations across the country, of which seven were
CRBC stations. There was broadcasting on the CRBC network in French and English.

The CBC

Parliament continued to take a close interest in broadcasting. After two more Parliamentary Committees on the
subject, it was decided to advance further.

With the passage of the Canadian Broadcasting Act in
November, 1936, the three-man Commission was replaced by
a new body, the Canadian Broadcasting Corporation. The
Corporation was provided with a General Manager, and
Assistant General Manager and a Board of nine Governors,
appointed by the Governor General in Council, which, in
effect, means that they were appointed by the government of
the day.

The CBC was to report to Parliament through the newly-
created Department of Transport. Its first General Manager
was an experienced British radio man, Gladstone Murray.
First chairman of the CBC Board of Governors was Leonard
W. Brockington, Q.C. The CBC was to be similar to the
BBC but with several major differences: (1) the CBC would
accept advertising programs; (2) private radio stations
would continue in operation, under the jurisdiction of the
CBC. Certain private stations would form part of the CBC
network, in order to extend the coverage of the national
service without the necessity of the heavy capital expenditure that would be required if all stations were owned
and operated by the CBC. The CBC was to be responsible
for the overall supervision and control of all private broadcasting stations.

The original Governors of the CBC were all part-time.
The Chairman received an annual honorarium of $1,500,
members of the executive committee were paid $1,000, and

the other governors received $50 per meeting and not more than $500 per annum, plus expenses.

The CBC was given power to borrow money, within limits, a power the Commission had lacked. The CBC was a far more formidable and autonomous organization than the Commission, but it still had far less autonomy and freedom than the BBC. Unlike the BBC, which operated under a 10-year charter, the CBC had to depend for both current expenditures and capital works on annual grants from Parliament.

In 1961, the CBC celebrated its 25th birthday. In that quarter century, much had been accomplished. In 1936, there were three important jobs to be done: (1) to extend radio coverage to Canadians in all parts of the country; (2) to provide a national service with a high proportion of Canadian programs; and (3) to provide opportunities for Canadian talent.

All of this could be accomplished in a country of vast distances and small, scattered population, only by great expenditure of effort and money.

To improve coverage, a series of high-powered 50,000 watt transmitters was planned. The first two came into operation in 1937 in Toronto and Montreal; not only did they cover these important cities, but the powerful signals covered wide rural areas beyond the limits of the cities. By 1939 regional transmitters of 50,000 watt power had been established in Saskatchewan and in the Maritimes.

It was decided that a country so vast that it extends across six time zones would best be handled by regions. Five broadcasting regions were established: British Columbia, the Prairies, Ontario, Quebec, the Maritimes. When Newfoundland became part of Canada in 1946, it became the 6th CBC region.

More listeners were now available for the national service. Programming could be done on a regional basis. The number of hours devoted to national network programs more than doubled. The emphasis on Canadian programs led to the development of the CBC National News Service. Once dependent on the newspaper wire services, the CBC now developed its own reporters and foreign correspondents, writers, announcers and commentators. Programs for farmers were developed including the National Farm Radio Forum, which has been studied by UNESCO and adapted in several other countries. School broadcasts were inaugurated. Coverage was provided for the Royal Tour in 1939.

The program policy placed emphasis on bringing the best of Canadian talent to the listeners via the national service. But, from the first, the CBC also brought into Canada the best of the programs offered by the United States networks, and the best programs available from Britain and other countries.

From 1944 to 1962 there were two English-language radio networks, so that listeners could have alternative programs. These were the Trans Canada Network, and the Dominion Network. The dependence on private stations is indicated by the fact that only the key station of the Dominion Network belonged to the CBC; coast to coast coverage was provided by 34 private stations. The Trans Canada Network consisted of 6 CBC stations and 28 private stations. The French radio network was composed of 3 CBC stations and 10 private stations.

The vast distances to be covered in order to provide Canadians with a national radio and TV system is illustrated by the fact that it cost the CBC more than $9 million in 1960 to pay for the 25,000 miles of network facilities required to link its various stations together.

The war presented special problems and many challenges. The CBC was a valuable factor in uniting Canadians behind the war effort, and keeping them fully informed about the dramatic events of the war years. During the years of war the CBC matured in experience, in national stature and acceptance.

With the war over, there were new challenges to be met. Most important was the development of an entirely new medium—television. But, even before that chapter opens, there were developments in radio. In 1947, the CBC Wednesday Night series was launched, bringing a rich and varied evening of cultural offering to interested listeners.

In 1945, the CBC began the operation of an International Service for the Government of Canada. The International Service now provides regular broadcasts in 15 languages for 30 countries abroad. The programs originate in the CBC studios in Montreal and are transmitted from special, high-power short-wave stations in New Brunswick. This is the Voice of Canada, speaking to the world.

In 1952, the CBC French network extended westward to connect with a private French station at Edmonton. In 1954, the CBC French station at Moncton went into operation.

Television

With the end of the war, television began a rapid boom in the United States. Many Canadians purchased sets to watch United States stations and complained about the tortoise pace with which Canada was moving into TV. The matter was considered by the Massey Commission, which recommended that the CBC should take the lead in the development of television.

In September, 1952, the first two CBC television stations went on the air in Montreal and Toronto. The government had decided that the CBC should provide a national service in TV, as in radio, and that it should establish its own TV stations in key centres before private licenses would be granted in these centres. In smaller communities, private licenses would be granted. Private stations would serve as affiliates of the CBC television network in locations where their coverage was required by the national service.

In January, 1953, there were two Canadian television stations in operation, both owned and operated by the CBC. There were about 225,000 TV receivers in use. A decade later, in January, 1963, there were 61 television stations in operation, 14 owned and operated by the CBC. Of 47 private TV stations, 33 were affiliated with the CBC national TV network. The number of television sets in use was over 4 million.

The Broadcasting Act of 1958

The year 1958 marked a turning point in broadcasting. In July, 1958, the wire and microwave network was completed between Victoria and Halifax making the CBC national service in television a reality. In that year, A. Davidson Dunton, who had guided the affairs of the CBC as Chairman of the Board of Governors, since 1945, resigned to take up the post of President of Carleton University. In 1958, Parliament, after deliberating the findings of the report which the Fowler Commission had submitted in 1957, brought in the first completely new broadcasting act since the founding of the CBC, the Broadcasting Act of 1958. The Royal Commission headed by Fowler had taken the trouble to draft, and include in their report, a proposed Broadcasting Act.

The Broadcasting Act of 1958 bore no resemblance whatsoever to the legislation suggested by the Royal Commissioners. It may have appeared to do so, since it did include a new regulatory body, the Board of Broadcast Governors, a title included in the Fowler Report. But the BBG created by the act of 1958 was *not* the BBG recommended in the Fowler Report. The name was the same, but it was a very different kind of rose.

With final authority over the issuing of licenses, the BBG quickly licensed second TV stations to private owners in major centres. It licensed other private TV stations. It authorized a private TV network. The CBC was given a TV license in Edmonton. The entire tone of television broadcasting began to change. Not all the blame can be laid at the doorstep of the BBG. The CBC can be challenged for meeting the competition of the private TV network with a battle of ratings, mounting its attack with a barrage of United States network and film programs in prime listening time.

The first private TV station to go on the air was CKSO-TV in Sudbury, launched in October, 1953. The private television network, CTV, began operations in the fall of 1961. Now, four out of five television stations in Canada are privately owned. Of three television networks, one is privately owned. Two networks, one in French and one in English are operated by the CBC, with heavy dependence on privately-owned affiliates. Early in 1963, application was made for a private French TV network.

The cycle is complete. At one time the private broadcasting stations feared that they might be eliminated by the national service. Now, it is the private broadcasters who are on the offensive.

X

AND FORWARD

AND FORWARD

The airwaves are a precious and limited natural resource; the uses to which they are put must be carefully guarded. Wavelengths occupied by stations or networks that fill them with canned and packaged rubbish are not available to inform, entertain and develop the taste of the people. What about the future? Whether or not the airwaves will, in the future, serve the many and varied needs of the Canadian people depends upon our ability to successfully meet a few important challenges to the broadcasting system. The challenges, in the main, concern organization, finance and the quality of programs.

The organization of broadcasting. We have inherited from the recent past a broadcasting system of mixed character, made up of public and private sectors. Within the public sector confusion has developed concerning the respective roles of the BBG and the CBC. It is up to the parliament of Canada to state the aims of the broadcasting system clearly and without ambiguity. Broadcasting legislation is required which will define the sphere of action and the responsibilities of each component or sector of the broadcasting system. Once the rights and responsibilities of each sector have been clearly defined, they must be firmly enforced in the public interest.

The economics of broadcasting. We know from experience and from frequent examination of our broadcasting system that we can only receive the benefits of an adequate national broadcasting service if we are willing to pay for that service. In this country of vast area and thinly-distributed population, the public must be prepared to supply funds, whether in the form of license fees on receiving sets, or from the public treasury.

Broadcasting is an expensive affair; this is particularly true for television. Revenue from advertising can help to meet the costs of the national broadcasting service, but the national service cannot be dependent on commercial revenue alone, anymore than could the school system, for example.

The national service. Every important study has underlined the fact that, because of the nature and distribution of our population, because of the territorial expanse of Canada and our proximity to the United States, the firm back-bone of our broadcasting system must be provided by a national public service. In addition to clearly defining the task of the national service which CBC-*Radio Canada* is to provide, parliament should also provide funds on a statutory basis and provide guarantees that will enable the corporation to carry out its task free from the dangers of political interference or pressure.

Stability and flexibility. All elements of broadcasting, public and private, need to work out satisfactory long-term plans. The elements needed for tomorrow's broadcasts cannot be quickly assembled. Artists, writers, producers and technicians must be recruited and trained. The buildings, electronic equipment, towers and transmission systems must be planned well in advance. There is merit in the oft-repeated recommendation that the CBC should have its tasks defined in a 10-year charter, and that its annual money needs should be provided by statute for that period.

Broadcasting is still a new, rapidly-changing medium. While the broad lines of future development must be clearly drawn to provide the stability necessary to long-term planning, each element of the broadcasting system must be allowed a certain flexibility to meet the inevitable changes demanded by a dynamic medium, in the framework of a revolutionary technology.

The private broadcaster. There is an important, established place for the private broadcasting station in the Canadian scheme of things. The private station provides an acknowledged community service; it may also serve its local audience, as a CBC affiliate, by distributing the programs of the national service. The private television network is in a position to add to the variety of program-fare available to viewers, by providing an alternative schedule to that of the national television service.

As we have seen, regulations have been developed over the years which require the broadcaster to meet certain standards of service, as a condition of the grant of a license by the BBG. Evidence has also accumulated that these regulations have not always been respected by the broadcaster, nor has their breach always resulted in action by the broadcasting authority.

The license issued to the private broadcaster gives him no proprietary interest in the airwaves. The license to operate a private broadcasting station is a publicly assigned privilege, granted on the condition that certain services will be provided to the public. In the future, as in the past, we have a right to expect that the performance of each broadcaster will be reviewed at regular intervals and that the license will only be re-issued where performance warrants it. Present regulations provide for short-term suspension of broadcasting privileges, for serious infraction. The possibility of cancellation of a broadcasting license, where warning action fails to bring about an improvement, should be considered.

The programs. The concern over the organisation, regulation and economics of broadcasting has but one motive. The test of the worth of each unit in the broadcasting system, whether it be a small-town station or a national network, is the schedule which it offers. Each unit in Canadian broadcasting has a responsibility to provide a varied, well-balanced schedule of programs for the eyes and ears of the Canadian audience.

It is by no means easy to provide a definition of what is "good Canadian broadcasting". We have seen some of the difficulties involved in the effort to provide for Canadian content and character through regulations and fixed percentage quotas. We know what we want: we want each broadcaster to provide a variety of programming so that the needs and interests of a highly diversified population will be reasonably met; we want program schedules which will enable the people of this country to know each other better, and enable them to see the world through Canadian eyes; we want opportunities for Canadian talent.

We want a broadcasting system that provides a good variety of high quality Canadian programs. We will get it only if the spirit as well as the letter of the law contained in the regulations is respected. If the broadcaster does not operate in the proper spirit, there is hardly any regulation, or set of regulations, governing quality, variety, Canadian content and character that cannot be rendered meaningless. No license should be granted or renewed unless the licensee maintains a proper balance through sustaining programs, makes use of local live talent, provides for the discussion of public issues and eliminates advertising excesses.

Broadcasting awards. In order to achieve good Canadian broadcasting, high standards of programming must be established. Well-aimed praise for good programs and specific criticism of bad programs are essential to the maintenance of standards.

A number of broadcasting awards exist now in Canada, but none with national recognition and stature. Perhaps it is to the Canada Council that we should turn for the establishment of a series of annual awards of merit in broadcasting. These awards could apply to networks, individual stations, producers, writers, actors and even to technicians. They could encourage imagination, initiative and high standards of performance. It would be useful if there were awards for stations in small communities operating with moderate resources, as well as for the big stations in metropolitan centres and for the national networks with greater resources of finance, facilities and personnel.

Regular review of Canadian broadcasting. In Britain, a regular review of broadcasting takes place at least every ten years, prior to renewal of the charter of the BBC. There has been no shortage of investigations into broadcasting in Canada. But these do not always take place when they are most needed. Nor does specific action always result. A case in point is the Royal Commission on Broadcasting of 1957, the recommendations of which were largely ignored. Another Royal Commission might be desirable at this time to take up where the last one left off. Instead of intermittent Parliamentary Committees, we might be better served by a Standing Committee on Broadcasting.

Undoubtedly there are a number of methods to be explored for the regular examination and overhaul of the Canadian broadcasting system. But the interest and participation of an informed public is the main basis upon which a brighter future for broadcasting can be assured. Writing a letter of commendation or disapproval to your broadcast service or station will not usher in the millenium, but it is now just as important a technique of democratic living as writing that traditional 'letter to the editor' or to your member of parliament.

The decisions made about our Canadian way of broadcasting in the months ahead could establish the pattern for a decade, even a generation. In our hands rests the responsibility to determine that the great powers of broadcasting will serve the needs of all Canadians for enrichment and education.

FURTHER READING

Much of the long debate on broadcasting in Canada is recorded in official publications. These are obtainable from any university or reference library, or from the Queen's Printer, if still in print.

Two royal commissions dealt exclusively with broadcasting:

Report of the Royal Commission on Radio Broadcasting, 1957 (*The Aird Report*);

Report of the Royal Commission on Broadcasting, 1957 (*The Fowler Report*).

A royal commission on culture devoted an important part of its deliberation to broadcasting. See the Report of the Royal Commission on National Development in the Arts, Letters and Sciences, 1949-1951 (*The Massey Report*). Chapter 3 of the report deals with broadcasting.

The Report of the Royal Commission on Government Organization, 1963 (*The Glassco Report*), Vol. IV, contains a section on the CBC.

Additional material will be found in reports of the numerous Special Parliamentary Committees on Broadcasting, and in debates on broadcasting in *Hansard*.

See also the annual reports of the Canadian Broadcasting Corporation and the Board of Broadcast Governors.

Occasional articles on broadcasting will be found in *Canadian Forum* and *Queen's Quarterly*.

News of broadcasting and popular articles are to be found in two trade papers, *The Canadian Broadcaster* and *Canadian Sponsor*, both published in Toronto.

Beginning in the 1930's, a considerable literature has been growing up around the topic of communications, a term which has come to be identified with the mass media and their influence.

Scholars in the United States have emphasized the sociological and psychological approach. See works by Walter Lippmann, Paul F. Lazarsfeld, S. I. Hayakawa, Gilbert

Seldes, Bernard Berelson, Wilbur Schramm, Charles A. Siepmann, Joseph T. Klapper and Harold D. Lasswell. The FCC "Blue Book" (*Public Service Responsibilty of Broadcast Licensees,* 1946) has set the standard in the United States for better programmes. The Commission's present programming policy is reflected in the publication, "Network Programming Inquiry: Report and Statement of Policy (FCC 60-970), *The Federal Register,* Washington, August 3, 1960.

Two Canadian scholars have raised historical and philosophical questions about the nature and influence of the mass media of communications. See the writings of Harold A. Innis and Marshall McLuhan.

A source of international information is UNESCO, Paris. The division of Mass Communications, UNESCO, produces a steady stream of books and pamphlets on many aspects of the mass media.

GLOSSARY

BBG   Board of Broadcast Governors, a government body dealing with the issue of licenses and the regulation of broadcasting for public and private stations and networks in Canada.

CAB   Canadian Association of Broadcasters, the body which represents most of the private broadcasting stations, both radio and TV. It was founded in 1926 and reorganized in 1931. For a number of years it was known as CARTB—Canadian Association of Radio and Television Broadcasters. With it are linked several regional associations of broadcasters: WAB—Western Association of Broadcasters; CCBA—Central Canada Broadcasters' Association; ACRTF—*Association Canadienne de Radio et Télévision de Langue Française;* and AAB—Atlantic Association of Broadcasters.

CBC   Canadian Broadcasting Corporation, a publicly owned organization established to provide national service in radio, and from 1952, in television. Known in French as *Société Radio Canada* or simply, as *Radio Canada.*

CTV   The CTV Television Network Ltd., the private Canadian television network.

D. of T. Department of Transport of the Federal Government deals with technical problem of broadcasting, and issues licenses on the advice of the BBG.

BBC   British Broadcasting Corporation, public, non-commercial broadcasting service in radio and television.

ITA   Independent Television Authority, provides an alternative British television service through contracts with commercial programming companies.

FCC   Federal Communications Commission, the official
           body responsible for issuing broadcasting licenses
           and regulating all broadcasting activities in the
           United States.

AM   Amplitude Modulation radio, the regular radio
           with us since the 1920's.

FM   Frequency Modulation radio, a later development
           designed to reduce interference and improve the
           quality and range of sound through a type of
           transmission that is based on variations in the
           frequency. A separate type of radio receiver is
           required.

Network—such as CBC in Canada, or Columbia Broad-
           casting System in the United States; a group of
           stations linked to carry a particular schedule of
           programs.

Satellite
station —in both radio and television, the range of a
           station or network can be extended by the use
           of unmanned transmitters. In radio they are
           known as low power relay transmitters. In tele-
           vision they are referred to as rebroadcasting sta-
           tions or network relay stations. These stations are
           generally linked by wire to the "parent" station.
           They make it possible to secure coverage in
           remote areas, and in pockets which, for geo-
           graphical reasons, are cut off from regular broad-
           casting signals.

Video
tape   —electronic tape upon which a television program
           is recorded for rebroadcast.

Micro-
wave   —an alternative to cable as a link between television
           stations.

INDEX

INDEX

127

130